Evolution of Design

100 Step-by-Step Case Studies
of Logo Designs and How They Came to Be.

David E. Carter
Editor

Art Direction Book Company
New York City

Art Direction Book Co.
10 E. 39th St.
New York 10016

Library of Congress Catalog Card Number 83-73399
ISBN: 0-88108-005-5

3

About the editor

David E. Carter has produced more books on trade mark design and corporate identity than anyone else in the world.

His previous volumes include:

The Book of American Trade Marks, 8 volumes
Letterheads Annual, 4 volumes
Corporate Identity Manuals
Designing Corporate Symbols
Designing Corporate Identity Programs
for Small Corporations

As president of David E. Carter Corporate Communications, based in Ashland, Kentucky, he has managed identity projects for small businesses as well as industrial giants.

He is a Clio-winning designer and has received more than 300 awards from some of the top advertising shows in the nation.

He has conducted seminars for *Advertising Age* on corporate identity, and now gives several two-day seminars on the topic each year.

He is a graduate of the University of Kentucky School of Journalism and holds a master's degree from Ohio University.

Contents

Nearly every company mark (or logo) ever designed evolved into its finished form. The actual evolution may have been a quick one-step process, or it may have been quite a complex procedure.

In this book, a number of corporate marks are shown—the designers have provided the material to demonstrate the step-by-step progression of those marks. The comments that accompany the designs are made by the designer of the mark.

This material should be of interest to designers, who can see how other designers have approached the design process. It should also be of benefit to clients, who can see that "that simple design" actually evolved with a great deal of thought behind it.

In preparing this book, I contacted a number of designers, asking their submissions for the publication. I sought variety—geographically, as well as in type and work appearing in this volume. Without their cooperation, this book would not have been possible.

This project is an image program for a regional CBS affiliate station.

Jefferson-Pilot Broadcasting retained Design/Joe Sonderman, Inc. to provide an updated and contemporary image for WBTV of Charlotte, North Carolina. The television station was an area leader in the industry and desired a fresh and progressive approach to its image. Design applications ranged from broadcast and advertising to vehicles and news sets.

The station's channel, 3, was also a part of its image, and the previous logotype reflected the WBTV and 3 combination.

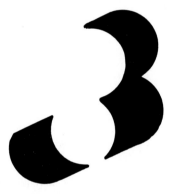

Many attempts were directed at symbols (stars, as an example)

or motion and activity (arrows), or the numeral 3. However the WBTV-3 combination still remained as a solid, yet undefined, solution. The client's close involvement helped to inforce this belief.

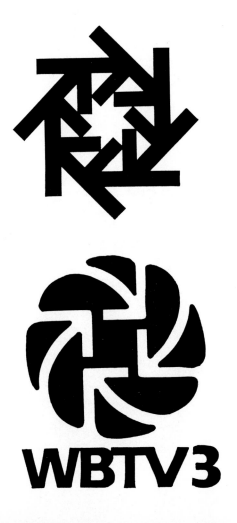

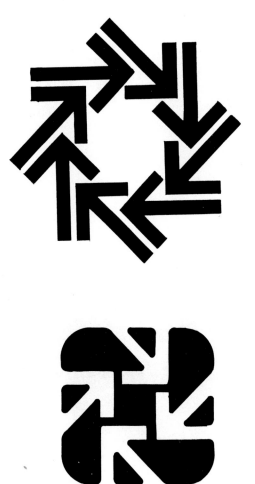

WBTV3

Therefore, the design task boiled down to "how can we create an image which blends numerals and letters, which is a successful transition from our previous logo?"

After several attempts, the logo took shape while experimenting with positive and negative shapes. Consideration was given to print media vs. broadcast media - quality gain or loss due to various forms of reproduction.

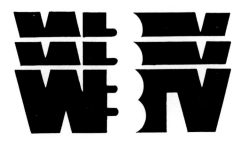

Designer: Joe Sonderman, Charlotte, North Carolina
Client: Jefferson Pilot Broadcasting/WBTV, Charlotte, North Carolina

The problem: to create a logo for Wavelink, a broadcasting communications system using fiber optics, to be used on the product cover, as well as in promotional advertising. It was necessary that the logo depict the product.

Getting the initial concept on paper

Letter style development

wavelink

Further lettering development

Final concept/solution, depicting fiber optics as well

wavelink
FIBER OPTIC COMMUNICATIONS

Designer: LeeAnn Brook, Nevada City, California
Client: Grass Valley Group, Inc.

This project was to create a symbol for a small commuter airline, so that when it was seen on the tail of the plane in another city it would visually depict the name of the airline.

Rough concept of tree and bird

A more graphic representation

Refining the graphics

Alteration of design

Designer: LeeAnn Brook, Nevada City, California
Client: Nevada County Aviation

National Memory Systems Corporation of Livermore, California retained Hartung & Associates to create the image for this newly established company. NMSC is a high-tech company involved in assembling memory systems for large corporations.

Our objectives were:
1. High tech
2. Futuristic (progressive)
3. Stable
4. Would possibly be identified by the initials "NMSC"
5. Non-tangible

We felt that the linear look would best represent NMSC.

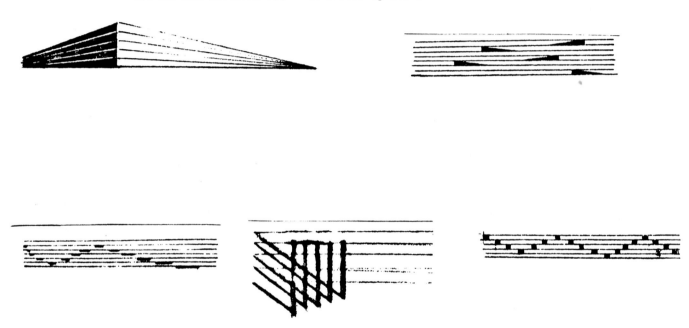

Computer memory systems supplied bits of information almost like musical notes on a scale. We talked about this approach; we liked it, but felt that its application on different elements (memory units, packages, etc.) would be difficult.

We also were working on a type style that would possibly work as one unit. Here we liked the type but not the element it was sitting on. The type has achieved one objective: it highlights NMSC.

Working with the same type, we moved to a linear look with movement in different directions.

National Memory Systems Corporation

The client said that it looks too much like this unit inside the larger unit.

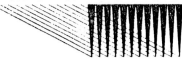

This was what we came up with and presented to the client. Also listed are some of the objectives that this mark has met.

National Memory Systems Corporation

1. NMS (C) highlighted.
2. Dimension
3. Gives a feeling of space even though it is on the same plane. (moving ahead)
4. Has an optical illusion effect.
5. Plays with your eye.
6. Lines indicate individual elements that come together to form a platform that the memory system sits on.
7. Rods cast a shadow that is an image (memory).
8. Looks modern; has a futuristic feeling.
9. Movement-oriented.

Since the client and we agreed that it did look somewhat tangible, we went back to work with a few more objectives:
1. It should now highlight NMS, not NMSC, as the client pointed out that NMSC was close to another company in his field.
2. We wanted to keep the same feeling of the mark, without giving it the look of a tangible object.

This looked interesting, version A

Possible pyramid showing stability and energy

Not quite there yet

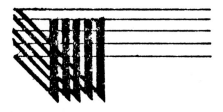

Possible if it is not so long like version A

Below is the mark, but this different type style doesn't look as good; back to the original style.

Designer: Hartung & Associates Ltd., San Ramon, California
Client: National Memory Systems Corporation

The following series of roughs, notes and ideas led to the development of a logo design for a Chicago-based real estate firm. Requirements of the logo were simplicity, visual recognition of the company's market involvement and the impression of growth.

During the initial client meeting, a rough sketch was rendered in an effort to establish the simple, basic message of shelters.

The initial sketch provided an avenue of exploration that led to the following concepts.

A simple rooftop image was too spartan, while multiple rooftops began to look like other nonrelated corporate logos.

With the addition of chimneys and windows, it became apparent that these elements could be arranged in a fashion that would be visually interchangeable, thus providing the logo with its needed character.

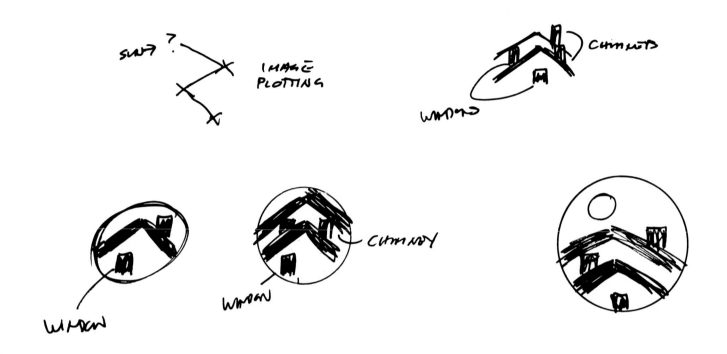

By using an image plotting concept and placing the sun in the sky, the initial design requirements were achieved with the final logo design.

Designer: Theodore C. Alexander, Jr., Chicago, Illinois
Client: Sharpe & Company, Chicago, Illinois

Shrimp and other crustaceans are the primary seafood products. The evolution of this design began with a shrimp. The following metamorphosis took place:

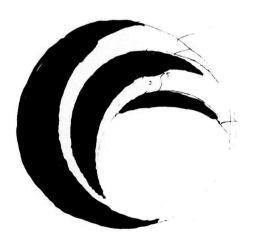

The "clamshell" was explored as being a bit more tolerable than the shrimp shape or its subsequent abstractions.

After exhausting reims of clamshells, a fish-like shape evolved in the form of a nautical flag and was seriously considered as the final identity for the client.

But because the fish market is just a percentage of their overall business, the designers were asked to explore a more appropriate symbol.

HumanGraphic then decided to use the wave shape the word "crest" refers to.

The result was an energetic "C" shape with some reference to crustacean characteristics originally pursued.

Designer: HumanGraphic, San Diego, California
Client: Crest International, Inc.

The La Jolla Development Company decided to change its faceless image by retaining HumanGraphic to develop a new symbol that best represents their name.

Geometric images relating to the square were studied singularly referring to parcels of land.

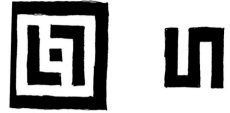

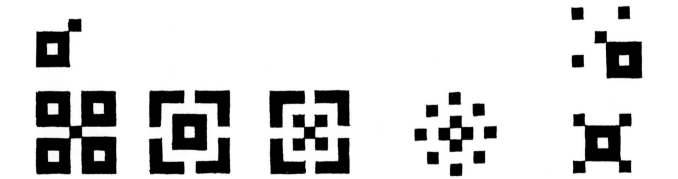

In many cases, the "L," "LJ" or "LDJ" were used and, for the most part, in a self-containing square format.

Because the name is long, any geometry that had any reference to the "L" was pursued.

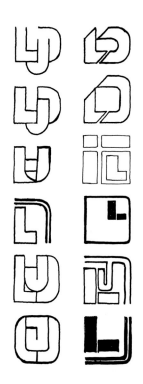

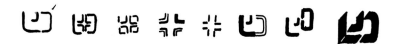

The resulting mark represents the dimensionality of their commercial buildings, and a subtle reference to beachside La Jolla by a curved shape.

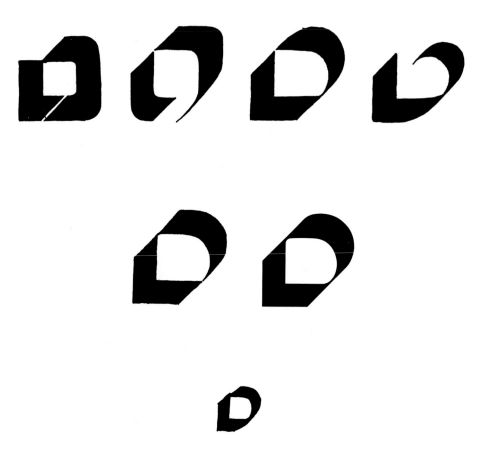

The "L" and "D" logo has positioned itself well amidst the competition.

Designer: HumanGraphic, San Diego, California
Client: La Jolla Development Company

A new company with a long, unchangeable name.

The design was initiated with the following representative words in mind:
Neptune, propeller, flagship, nautical, Viking, wake, bow, stern, etc.

The resulting chronology is a study that eventually found its way to a "C" shape (no pun intended) conformation. The mark represents a bow cutting through water.

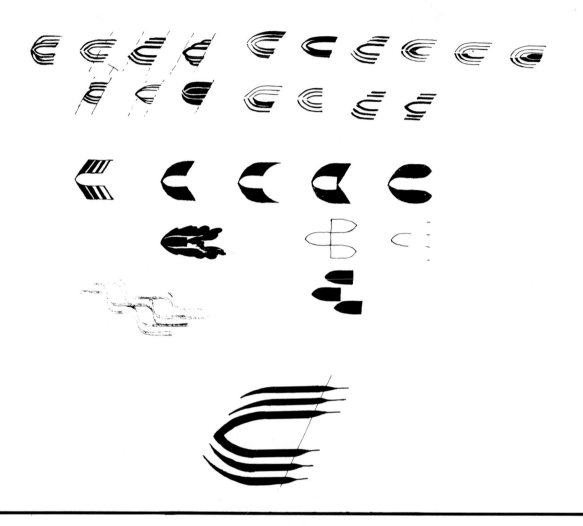

The stationery format utilizes the angle of the mark to evoke a feeling of nautical flags.

Designer: HumanGraphic, San Diego, California
Client: Crutchfield Yacht & Ship Brokers

Kelly and Duva was a new partnership, and both partners took an active role in the development of their new mark.

A dollar sign on the move.

Kelly & Duva with focus on the ampersand in the form of a dollar sign.

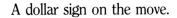

Kelly & Duva wanted to try the bronze plaque impression and to have this double as an actual bronze sign.

The typical pie-chart was used to develop cut sections to form the shape of a "K." The partner, Nick Duva, wondered if the backward "D" shape did not obscure his half of the pie.

After much more discussion, turning the pie sections into other combinations, reviewing sketches by the client and their wives, and acknowledging the importance of having both the "K" and the "D" equally displayed, HumanGraphic embarked on a more definitive representation of the letterforms.

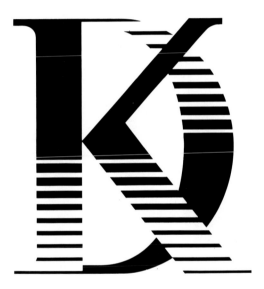

The final result was the "K" overlapping the "D" with both letterforms sharing a common "spine". The merging of the two letterforms were further integrated by using graduated horizontal lines.

Designer: HumanGraphic, San Diego, California
Client: Kelly and Duva

With the growth of a very profitable product and a move to a new facility, the company president initialed this change in identity.

The problems were obvious. Too tight letterspacing in the old logotype made it difficult to read, negative areas disappeared when the logotype was reduced or was displayed on the electronic screen. But the problem was to maintain whatever "equity" the old logotype had and to transfer that onto the new.

The following chronology shows a metamorphosis from the old to the new:

Hyspan with the capital "H" was agreed to as an important change.

The cap "H" allows the impression to be less of a product image than that of a corporate image. Emphasizing various letterforms helps determine pronunciation of the name, and brings more characteristic reference to the words "high" and "expansion."

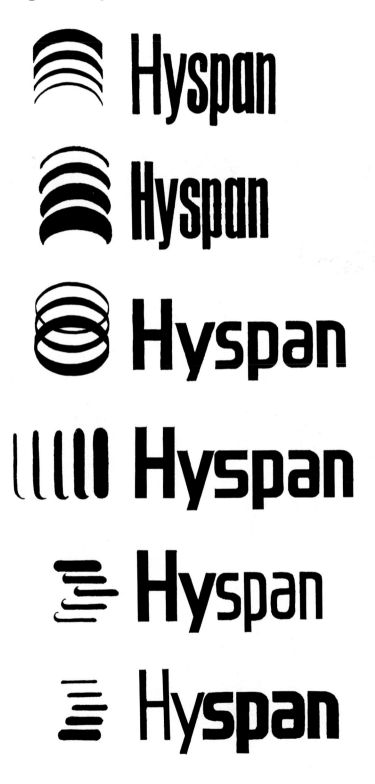

The logotype eventually evolved into a non-condensed typestyle for easier reading, better legibility, and compatibility with the "corporate typestyle".

Hyspan

Hyspan

Hyspan

The development of a symbol was necessitated by acknowledging the need for a "punctuation" to the word and graphically substantiating the literal effect the name has. Consequently, a variation of expansion joint images were created, but abstracted, to avoid alienating the other products presently sold or soon-to-be developed.

The result was an easily applied, contained symbol and a versatile logotype.

Designer: HumanGraphic, San Diego, California
Client: Hyspan, Inc.

Robinson Excavating was an established company that wanted a new look. We presented these logo roughs.

The mark at left was selected, but the client wanted the name to be larger, and also wanted a different typestyle (Machine Bold was chosen).

Designer: David E. Carter Corporate Communications, Inc., Ashland, Kentucky
Client: Robinson Excavating

39

When Owensboro Federal began opening branch offices in various cities, a name change was decided upon since the current name was just too geographically limiting. The name Cardinal Federal was chosen and work began on a new logo.

 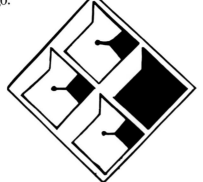 

A few of the roughs presented.

The client liked this concept — the negative space of a "C" forms a cardinal. We refined the mark to make the bird appear more like a cardinal.

First Choice

Second Choice

Third Choice

The client felt the mark overwhelmed the type and worked up these variations, noting their order of preference.

1

4

2

5

3

In steps one through three we drastically reduced the weight of the mark. In steps four and five we slightly reduced it. In all five cases the size of the type has been slightly increased in relation to the mark.

The client felt none of the changes were suitable and suggested the mark at left. Basically, we felt this destroyed our original design. We suggested that rather than attempt to achieve a balance between logo and type by reducing the weight of the logo, the best solution would be to increase the weight of the type. We presented the design at right, and — with the exception of shortening the cardinal's "tail" — it became the finished mark.

Designer: David E. Carter Corporate Communications, Inc., Ashland, Kentucky

Client: Cardinal Federal Savings & Loan Association

41

Anderson Federal Savings and Loan was branching out of their hometown and found their name too restrictive. The name "American Federal" was chosen.

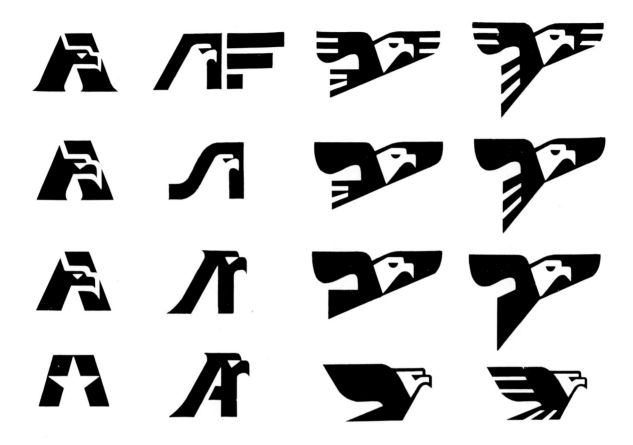

Since their previous logo had been an eagle, the client wanted the new logo to also feature an eagle. These marks were presented, and we selected our favorite to feature on various items (letterhead and envelope, signage, etc.).

Our favorite mark (right) and the rough sketch from which it developed.

The client felt this mark was too similar to the one used by the U.S. Postal Service, and it was decided that anything in profile would probably be rejected for the same reason. Also, a full view of an eagle would maintain more of the equity from the Anderson Federal logo.

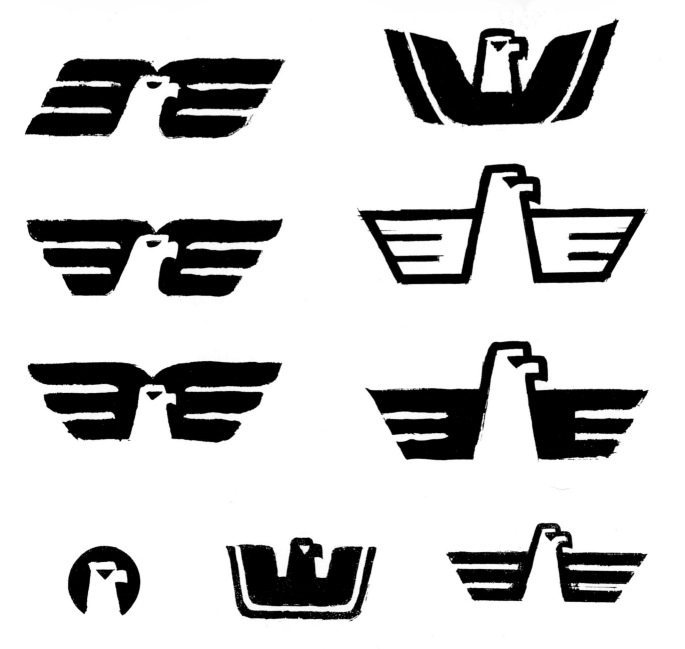

These pencil sketches were presented, and the final mark was developed
from the lower right-hand rough.

American Federal
Savings & Loan Association

Designer: David E. Carter Corporate Communications, Inc., Ashland,
        Kentucky
Client: American Federal Savings & Loan Association

Three Ohio savings and loans were merging, and required a new name and logo.

State Fidelity Savings **SFS**

FIRST FEDERAL SAVINGS

Merging institutions.

First phase: presented name with mark.

Second phase: alternate names and additional graphics for the first proposed name.

Mid★American

Third phase: proposed the name "Mid-American" and created graphics based on the flag. The name was later changed to "Mid-America" at the client's suggestion.

44

Mid★America Savings ▬▬

We added the word "Savings" on a second line, and introduced the bars to maintain balance and give a more flag-like appearance.

Mid★America Federal ▬▬

Mid★America Federal

Mid★America Federal

Mid★America Federal ▬▬

The two lines were staggered to give more visual dynamism. Also, it was felt the stripe through the star and the words was too distracting. "Savings" was changed to "Federal," and these four variations were presented.

Mid★America Federal ▬▬

Designer: David E. Carter Corporate Communications, Inc., Ashland, Kentucky
Client: Mid-America Federal

Our Lady of Bellefonte Hospital is an up-to-date medical facility sponsored by the Franciscan Sisters of the Poor.

The first group of marks presented to Our Lady of Bellefonte Hospital. We worked on themes of growth and renewal — thus the trees and crosses. Nothing here really struck the fancy of the Board of Directors.

A couple of marks from the second group presented. The client wished to see the mark at right altered so that it would more obviously appear to be a cross. We extended the lower portion (below).

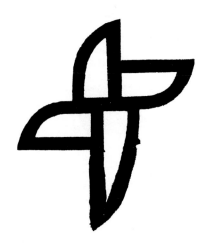

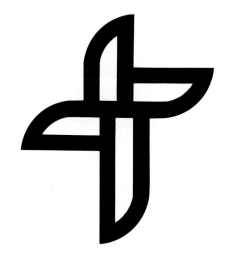

Since *Bellefonte* means "beautiful fountain" in French, the client felt that a fountain should be featured. At left is a combination of a fountain, a cross and a tree; and at right, a fountain alone. Neither of these designs was acceptable.

We continued to pursue the fountain theme and came up with the mark at right, which was approved.

Our Lady of
Bellefonte
Hospital

In the meantime there was an administrative change at the hospital, and it was decided to return to the cross theme.

Designer: David E. Carter Corporate Communications, Inc., Ashland, Kentucky
Client: Our Lady of Bellefonte Hospital

47

A.B. Dick Products Company of West Virginia decided it was time to change their name — since the company was becoming more and more geared toward distributing modern office technology, and no longer wanted to be strapped with the image of a duplicator supplier. We were retained to develop both the new name and graphics.

First presentation of names and logos.

Second group presented. The names A.B.Tech and Office IQ were
eliminated.

The typestyle was changed from Franklin Wide Italic to Franklin Italic.

The client preferred the name "InfoTrax" and decided on this mark. Unfor-
tunately, "InfoTrax," which was originally cleared for use in the states involved, was upon further investigation found to be too similar to the name
of another company in the same product line.

49

Back to the beginning. New roughs were developed for the name Quorum
Corporation.

Quorum
Corporation

More roughs.

Quorum Corporation

Next, we presented these marks.

We also re-presented one of the marks we had originally proposed, along with further variations of the "Q" form.

The word "corporation" was dropped from the graphics and the mark was selected.

Designer: David E. Carter Corporate Communications, Inc., Ashland, Kentucky

Client: Quorum Corporation

Citizens Savings of Portsmouth, Ohio retained us to manage a name change project. Once the new name — Civic Savings — was chosen, we began the process of creating the logo.

We wanted a design that would reflect stability, yet would project the image of a modern, growing financial institution.

We did a number of roughs with an abstract style, but nothing here really excited us.

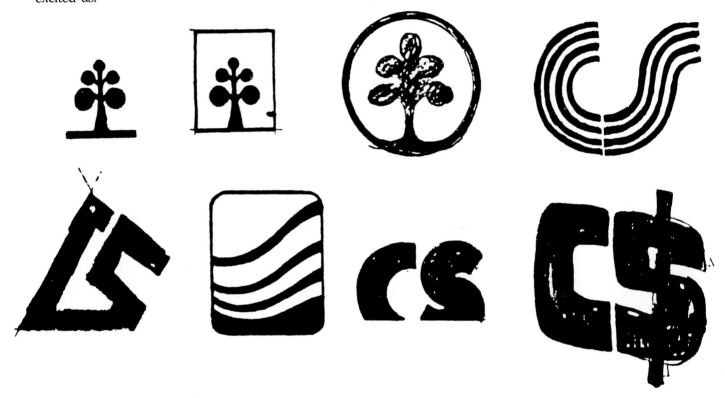

Feeling that "Civic" had positive Roman connotations, we did this rough featuring a distinctive type style and a medallion with a Roman bust.

Although we weren't 100% sold on any of the designs, we took all these rough (and others) so the client could see our progress.

54

The client shared our lack of enthusiasm for any of the designs. However, we all felt that the typography had definite possibilities.

When we viewed the type standing alone, other possibilities became apparent.

While in the client's office, we did several roughs.

CIVIC
SAVINGS

Noting the near-symmetry of CIVIC, we viewed the two "I's" as architectural columns.

This enlargement of the I's to form a column didn't work, but it did lead one step closer to our final solution.

This looked better, but the design was top-heavy.

The addition of the base gave us a mark with classic balance, a good image of stability—and with the "roof"—a very appropriate design for a financial institution whose primary purpose is to make home loans.

Designer: David E. Carter Corporate Communications, Inc., Ashland, Kentucky

Client: Civic Savings, Portsmouth, Ohio

Clinton County Farm Co-op of Frankfort, Indiana, decided their name was no longer appropriate, since many co-op members were located outside Clinton County.

A new name, AgMax, was selected and preliminary design work began. It was felt that the equity from their product mark for Country Fresh Feeds, which featured a red, orange and yellow sunrise, should somehow be retained.

We came up with these roughs — each based, to some degree, on the sunrise theme.

Other ideas based on the same color scheme. It was decided that the bars which contain concentric semi-circles were the more interesting; however, the design still seemed a little static.

The use of parallel angles made the design more dynamic.

These marks in finished form were among the first presented to the client.
The client was interested in the lower two marks, but wanted to see the
angles reversed.

These finished marks were also presented. The client wished to see another variation on the angles of the lower mark.

We presented the alternate designs the client had requested. We felt the extended angle on the lower mark weighed down the design, and the client agreed.

The approved mark. The name appears in black, and the bars are — from top to bottom — red, orange and yellow.

Designer: David E. Carter Corporate Communications, Inc., Ashland, Kentucky

Client: AgMax, Frankfort, Indiana

58

Rob was asked to describe his specialty and responded by indicating the following: Southern California Style, Energy Conscious, Personal and Fun.

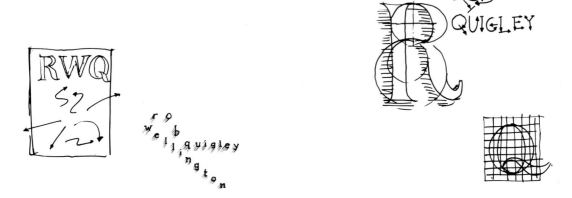

Many of the more pertinent preliminary sketches were lost or discarded. The few representative images shown here relate somewhat to the playfulness described by Rob. Some workable images that helped the ultimate direction were: shadows, hand-drawn arrows, the square grid, geometric constructions and Southern California palm trees.

The resulting mark was a typeface similarly drawn to look like Helvetica. The multiple vertical shapes are subtly broken into horizontal layers to help further indicate to the viewer a building concept. The shadows represent the energy aspect (i.e. solar energy). And finally, the long tall palm tree, typical of Southern California, as a contrasting punctuation to the Quigley name.

The mark successfully represents Rob's personality, and successfully positions this maverick architect among his peers.

Designer: HumanGraphic, San Diego, California
Client: Rob Wellington Quigley, AIA Architect

This project was to create a logo for The Pest Chaser, a product using ultrasonic sound waves to repel unwanted pests and insects. Logo would be used on the product cover, as well as on the packaging and promotional advertising.

Concept of repelling

Ideas on graphic representation

Type and graphic rough

Alternate idea

Further development

Designer: LeeAnn Brook, Nevada City, California
Client: Sonic Technology

After nearly a quarter century of health care service to Northern California, the Sisters of Mercy decided to redefine their mission through the unification of their four hospitals under one corporate entity. This redefinition called for the replacement of the Sisters' shield, which had also been serving in various forms as the identity for the hospitals. The new identity had to provide visual continuity throughout all communication elements for the holding company, all four hospitals, and their subsidiary organizations.

Because the identity had to represent a variety of diverse factions within the organization, we conducted extensive research, interviewing over 200 people and established design criteria. We decided that the identity should reflect:

1. warmth and compassion
2. a balance between the traditional and progressive
3. both the spiritual and medical character
4. quality and excellence.

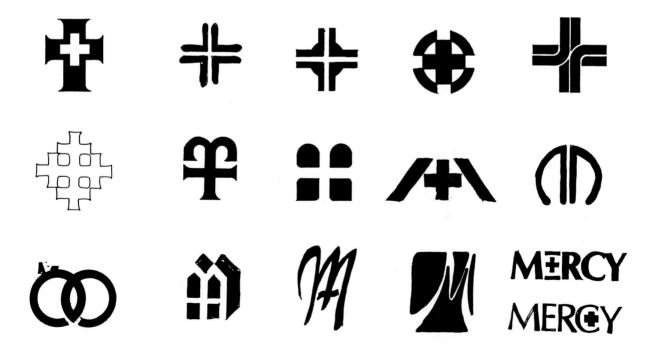

Once the design criteria were approved, we began working with the Sisters' shield. While we believed that the shield was too archaic to work as the identity alone, the Sisters and many others had very strong ties to it and asked us to present one solution that incorporated it. The solutions we developed with the shield confirmed our original belief.

We began working instead with the Sisters' maltese cross to reflect Mercy's religious heritage, using it in conjuction with the medical and red cross to portray these two key aspects of the organization's character.

Out of our attemps to represent the all-encompassing qualities of Mercy's commitment to the care of the total person as well as the community and employees, we experimented with the initial "M" and the word Mercy as a logotype. These solutions in themselves did not reflect the humanistic concerns of the organization that was central to the spirit of Mercy.

To infuse the symbol with a human quality, we tried using both the heart and the human figure in various combinations. Pulling elements from each step of the evolutionary process led us to the final design solution.

The circular enclosure symbolizes the Mercy heritage of caring not only as it encompasses the total needs of the patient but also as it reaches out to enfold those who work and live within the Mercy family. As the logo abstractly forms the initial "M," the right and left sides represent both the spiritual and medical concerns of the Mercy health care systems. The dual nature of Mercy's traditional spiritual values and progressive health care is further emphasized by the formation of the cross in the center comprised of both the medical red cross and the Christian cross.

Mercy
Health Care Organization

We selected the Optima typestyle because of its balance between progressive and traditional and the corporate colors of cinnamon and gray to enhance the warm character of the symbol.

Designer: Jane Burton·Wagstaff, Marketing by Design, Inc., Sacramento, California
Client: Sisters of Mercy

In the beginning of this project, we were working on a mark for Consolidated Fencing Incorporated.

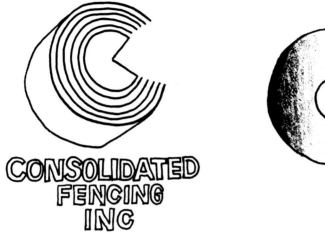

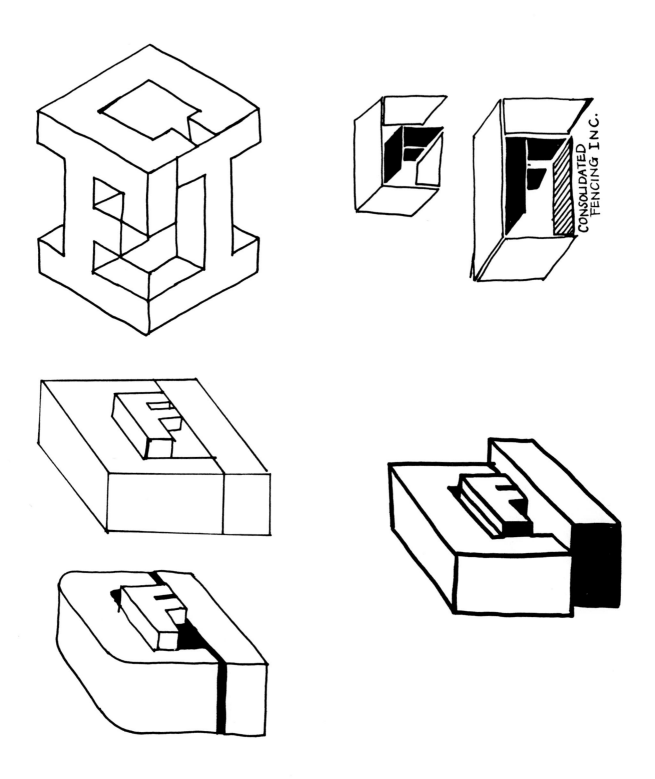

Part way through, the name was changed to Quikfence, a name that better describes the product of the company. It is a modular precast concrete fence system.

Our first explorations centered around the initials and the look of the system itself.

These are diagrams of the locking systems.

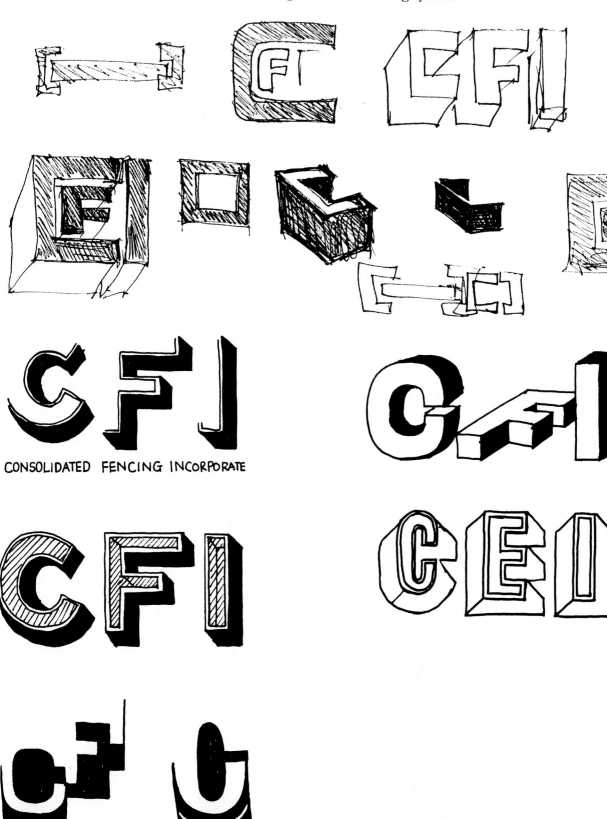

CONSOLIDATED FENCING INCORPORATE

One thing that bothered me about these is the letter "H" that keeps appearing strongly.

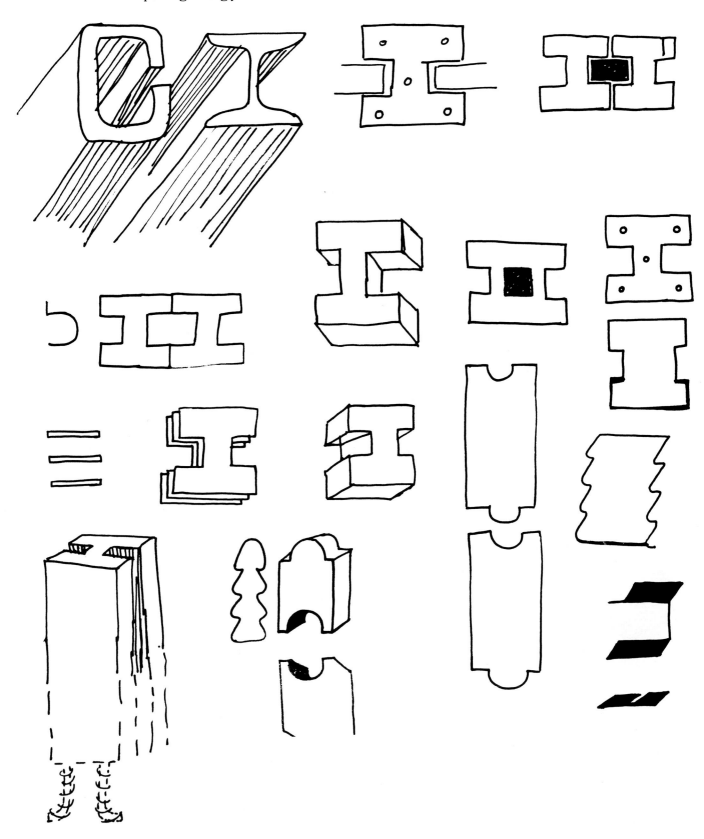

Most of these explore a "C" casting a shadow or trying to be very fence– or wall-like.

CONSOLIDATED
FENCING
INCORPORATED

CONSOLIDATED
FENCING INC

Some of these led to simple abstract walls.

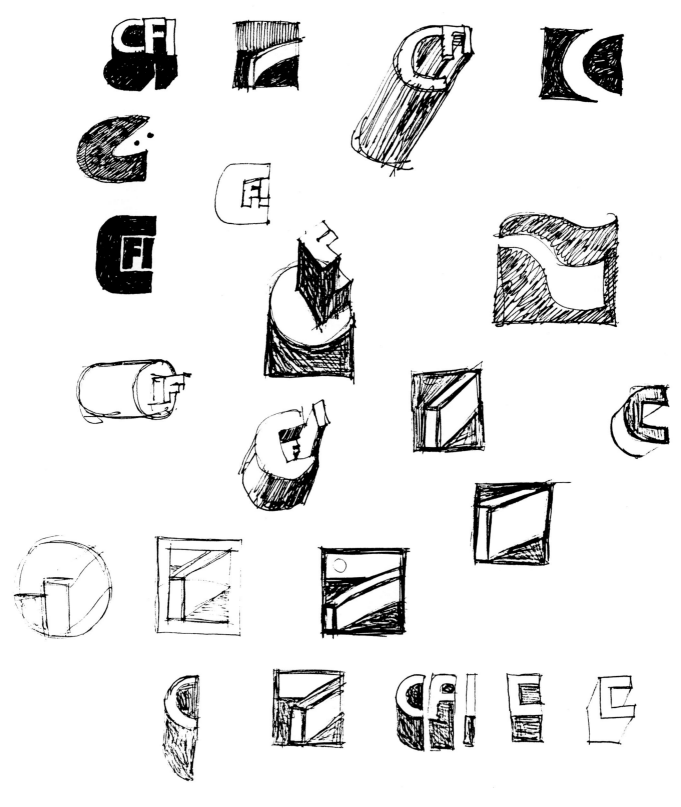

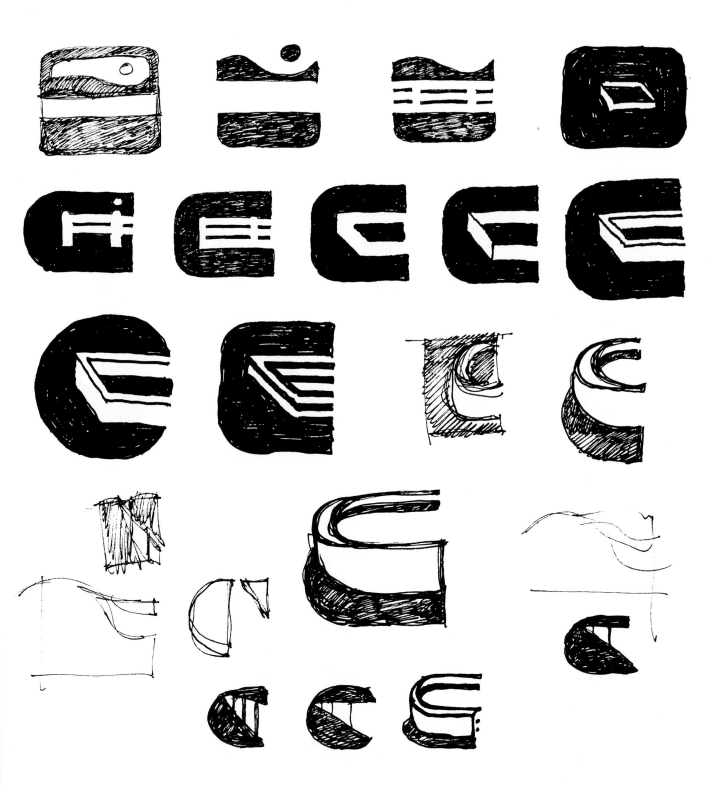

At this time we were told to work with the name "Quickfence" for the purpose of our mark, not CFI.

CONSOLIDATED FENCING INC

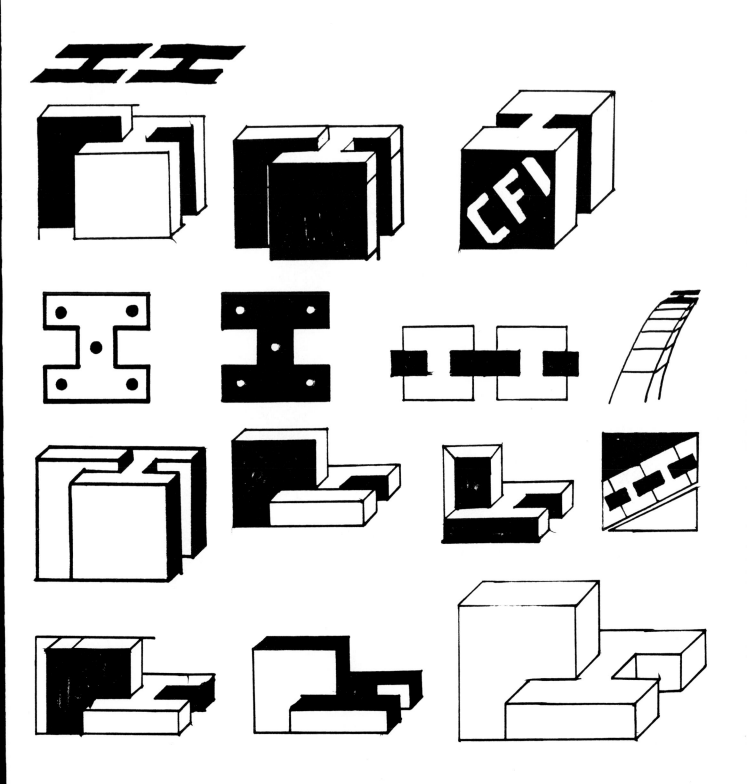

These are some first explorations with a "Q".

However, looking at the earlier explorations with an abstract wall, we saw how it could be used in a "Q". We changed the direction of the wall (tail of the Q) and experimented with the weights of the black areas.

77

We lettered the name in microgamma and Eurostyle because the character of those faces seemed to fit the look of our new "Q". We altered the "Q" and "K" of the typeset word. The finished mark and logotype as it was presented and used.

QUIKFENCE

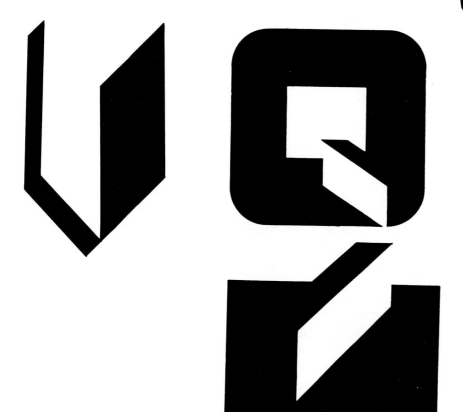

QUIKFENCE

Designer: Don Weller and Chikako Matsubayashi, Los Angeles, California

Client: Consolidated Fencing Incorporated

78

This project was to develop a logo that gives a new approach to representing a law practice.

Getting the possible concepts on paper

Graphically representing type concept

Furthering the graphics

Designer: LeeAnn Brook, Nevada City, California
Client: Nevada County Legal Aid

Ramos and Associates is a large architectural firm in Baja. The principal of the firm is dedicated to visual design; thus, he wanted a contemporary symbol that reflected his operation and goals. The preliminary designs had to deal with the letter "A," which is a company consideration in the distant future, and abstract, rigid designs that reflected structural components in buildings.

Two sets of drawings were submitted for approval. One of the earliest designs was selected for development. Eventually, this design was selected because it fulfilled the design criteria in the most ways.

Designer: Allan Miller, San Diego, California
Client: Ramos y Asociados Arquitectos, S.C.

Scotty's is a small retailer of homemade cookies baked from a special recipe.

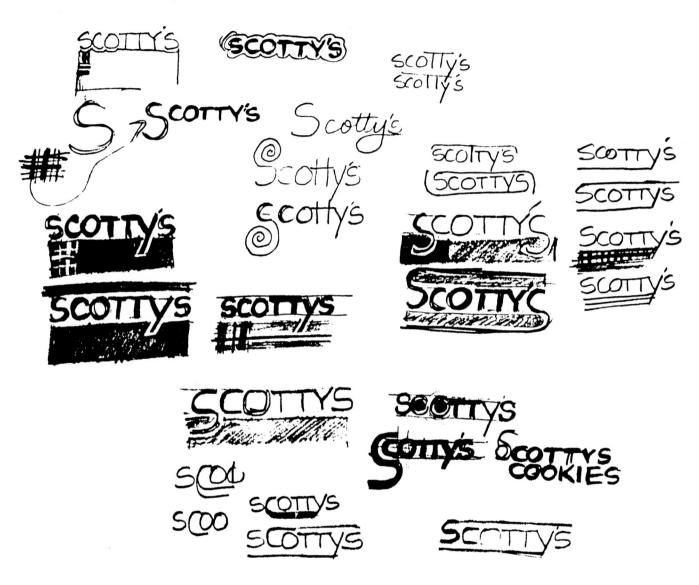

The preliminary explorative directions included some form of plaid design to reinforce the "Scotch" aspect of the client's name. However, as the project developed, it seemed that the emphasis should be placed on the name "Scotty's" itself in order to evoke a distinct name recognition for a new product line and store name.

The formal, rather rigid "Scotty's" logo gradually was transformed into a more informal and visually flowing symbol to reflect the informality of the products — snacks and desserts.

Further subtle transformations occured later as the word "homemade" was inserted and the "& Cookies" were included. The logotype was placed eventually into a rectangular background shape in order to give the name symmetrical geometric shape that would easily be fitted into the packaging and signage programs.

COOKIES

Designer: Allan Miller, San Diego, California
Client: Scotty's Cookies & Cheesecakes

Plaza Montesinos is a commemorative museum sponsored and designed by the Mexican government as a goodwill gesture. Padre Montesino was a 16th century cleric who tried to instill self-dignity and self-worth to the masses through spirited speechmaking. A statue of the cleric, approximately 70 feet high, is positioned atop the museum building. Its pose and form are captured by the pictorial symbol that acts as the trademark.

Since the museum required street signs for tourists, it was thought that a silhouette depicting the statue would be a logical visual connection with the museum site and facilitate guidance. Additionally, as the development progressed, it was indicated that the spirited qualities of Padre Montesino could not be easily depicted through abstract symbols as glyphs or similar marks. Thus, the pictorial representation evolved as the most appropriate for recognition and capturing the spirit of the theme.

The form of the cleric remained anonymous until the head of the huge sculpture was completed. Only then, after photos were received as references, did the form develop more as a representational shape. Some details were projected into the articulation of the hands to evoke a spirited gesture. The cross was a major design feature in order to immediately identify a religious personage. Additionally, the cowling of the priest was a major design feature from the beginning stages in order to further evoke recognition.

Plaza Montesinos

Designer: Allan Miller, San Diego, California
Client: Ministry of Public Works, Mexico

85

We were asked to design a logo for a company, The Network for Learning, that had just purchased an existing company, The Class Factory. This new company was to have a logo design based on the Class Factory's logotype and incorporating the Network's logotype.

the Class Factory, inc.

The existing type for Class Factory worked fairly well with the Network's typeface. Working to keep "The Class Factory" dominant in the design, because of its present recognition, we came up with these roughs.

The A NETWORK FOR LEARNING PROGRAM **Class Factory**

A NETWORK FOR LEARNING PROGRAM
class factory

class A NETWORK FOR LEARNING PROGRAM **factory**

class FOR LEARNING PROGRAM A NETWORK **factory**

The client liked the sketch including the rules and asked us to pursue that idea, but to replace "the" before Class Factory. The logo was also to be used as the masthead in a monthly catalog. Working with the rules, we presented these ideas.

The Class Factory
A NETWORK FOR LEARNING PROGRAM

A NETWORK FOR LEARNING PROGRAM
The Class Factory

A NETWORK FOR LEARNING PROGRAM
The Class Factory

After reviewing the various ideas, both we and the client agreed the logo worked best eliminating "the" before Class Factory and using bold face type for the Network. The final result exaggerated caps for the "C" and "F" in Class Factory, contrasting the big bold type with the fine hairline rules which disappear behind the bold logo.

A NETWORK FOR LEARNING PROGRAM
Class Factory

This is the existing logotype.

Designer: Adrienne Y. Carlin, AYC Graphics, New York, New York
Client: Network For Learning

One of our continuing clients, a medical center, retained us to create an identity for a new service called Comprehensive Rehabilitation Center. Its function was to provide all services—physical, emotional and social—to disabled persons. The director of the program was herself in a wheelchair, and she had definite ideas about the mark. She wanted something that would show mobility, and that could be used in a bright color. It was decided at the first meeting that the name was too unweildy and that the program would probably end up being referred to as the CRC. With this information we headed to the drawing board.

Our first thoughts were to use a wheelchair as the obvious symbol.

Our first attempt, was to incorporate the wheelchair as a part of the letters, the "c" being ideal as the vehicle. It was decided that the look was too static.

So we added action lines, and pulled the wheelchair off the letters for more action; it was okay.

We tried some variations, we liked the action lines better here, but felt that we were losing the wheelchair.

We were pretty happy with this solution, but felt that we should show the client more options. We had this on the wall for a few days.

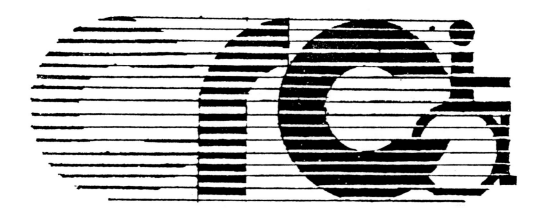

This refinement pleased us more, the forward lean on the figure begins to show more momentum and the absence of the drag lines makes the mark stronger.

We began to explore some alternatives, however, we were afraid this one would be too light.

This seemed pretty nice, though the speed lines didn't quite make it.

We began to play with the national symbol for the disabled, and tried to animate it.

This idea was a spin-off of the last, but a little too light.

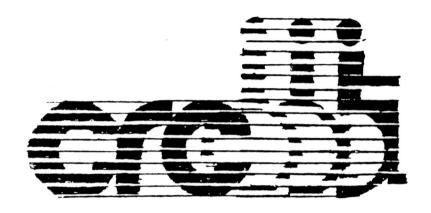

We decided to present this version.

As an alternate we went back and played about with the original idea.

This helped bold up the mark; we thought that with the addition of a legend this might work. But we were worried about identification of the CRC.

And came up with this. We thought the letterforms were a bit crude, and probably difficult to read.

We moved our wheelchair and gave it the action, refined the type and decided that we had solved the problem. Because of the prior history with the client this was the only mark that we actually presented. We sold it!

Designer: Gerry Rosentswieg/Thom Collins, Los Angeles, California
Client: Comprehensive Rehabilitation Center

The local Heart Association contacted us to provide the identification for a development program to raise money for research into heart disease. They had no ideas or parameters, except for the fact that the mark would be normally reproduced in two colors, black and heart red. It seemed easy, until we tried.

Our first thoughts were hearts and EKG tapes but we felt these were fairly hokey, and not especially good design.

We were afraid this one didn't say research.

So we tried this and we tried a medical approach, but it didn't say research.

This seemed to suggest lungs more than heart. Even though the idea started as a research flask.

Research

Research Research

We played with straight type, with a heart for embellishment.

And these were tried, but rejected as not being very clear.

The test tube and flask recurred and we liked these, but felt they were too light.

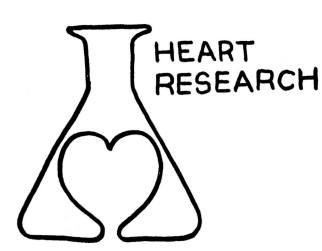

So we colored them in and reappraised everything that we had done. It seemed that the ideas were good, but that the tie into the Heart Association wasn't clear. We had the elements.

HEART
RESEARCH

So we put them together and solved the problem.

Designer: Gerry Rosentswieg, Los Angeles, California
Client: Los Angeles County Heart Association

Telematic manufactures and markets a variety of equipment that processes incoming and outgoing telephone calls. Its primary function is to simplify complex telephone systems.

The assignment called for a design that brought attention to the name "Telematic" and communicated the process of something complex becoming simple. Italic type added the speed. The rest was working out the type relationship and playing with thicks and thins of the lines.

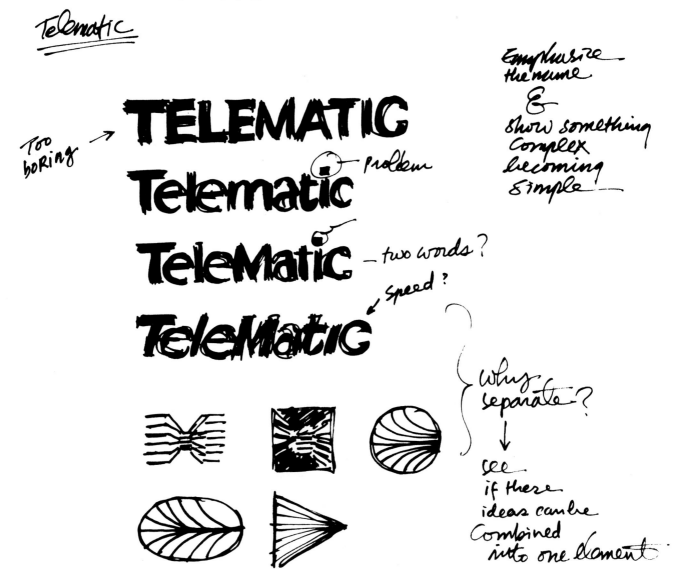

Because the name was short and simple, there was no need to add a trademark.

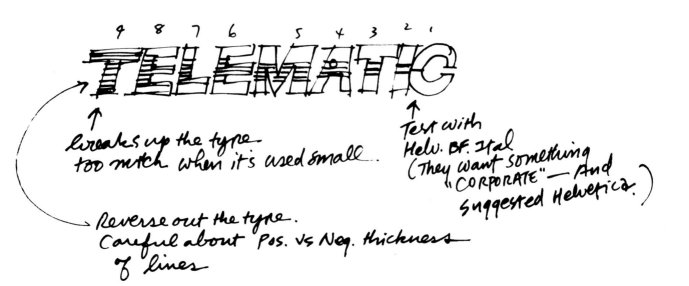

Not often, but sometimes, the first spontaneous idea can be the strongest idea.

I presented this idea only with the application of the letterhead, envelope and business card.

The client asked, "How soon can we have the stationery?"

Designer: Gene Davis & Associates, Seattle, Washington
Client: Telematic

We began developing a logo for Catalena Company by simply using the name within an attractive border.

From there on, we decided to work with a "c" or combination of two "c's".

After several very graphic approaches, our client felt he'd like to see incorporated a symbol representative of his trade; construction (such as a hammer, construction hat, or nail).

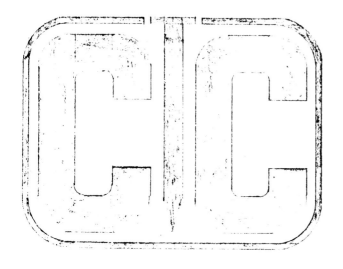

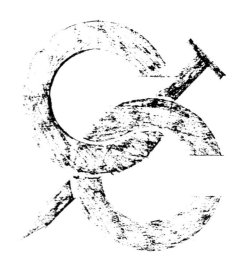

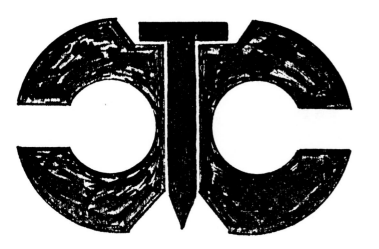

The nail lent itself to many different design ideas.

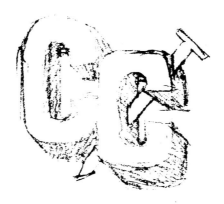

We thought that a blocky, solid "c" was a very appropriate choice for a company involved with construction.

The final logo is a little less complicated, but still retains a blocky, solid, firm look indicative of a construction company.

Designer: Tissa Porter Advertising, Bryan, Texas
Client: Catalena Company

East Hampton Green is a new residential development area.

The client suggested some kind of script lettering.

The next step was to visit the site and study the kind of houses that were being built. I learned that all houses were either Victorian or Salt Box style — all nostalgic houses. And, the logo application was limited to signs and a folder.

I did three designs. First, a script since they asked for it. But I added border lines to reflect the mood of the houses. Second design was to actually show the kind of houses they were building. Third, show more than one house as a development while emphasizing the name.

The client rejected all three. They didn't want the script anymore.

The next and final design was accepted with much enthusiasm. The concept was based on how to show nostalgic houses without showing houses.

All 33 houses were sold in a month. And 22 of them weren't even built.

Designer: Gene Davis & Associates, Seattle, Washington
Client: East Hampton Green

When we first began developing a logo for Warwick Investment Management, we tried different ways to interlock or link three initials. This didn't seem to bring out anything worthwhile.

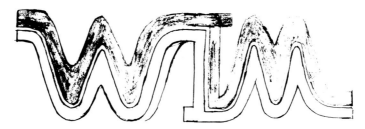

Since the monogram approach was not seeming to work, we opted for the trade symbol approach. After considering several ideas, the "graph" seemed to be the most workable.

The client liked the concept — "but investments are charted on bar charts," he said. Hence, the evolution of a "W" in the form of a bar chart.

After adjusting the width on the final art, we produced a logo which immediately identifies our client as distinctive and professional.

Designer: Tissa Porter Advertising, Bryan, Texas
Client: Warwick Investment Management

The designer was asked to develop a logo type to be used in a company-wide sales promotion. The overall theme was football, so it was suggested the type design have a "football" look.

The designer tried several approaches. The pentagram form was pursued because it suggests stardom which was appropriate for this promotion.

The type was narrowed down to the shadow face because of its similarity to varsity letters, which is consistent with the theme. The proportions and weights still had to be worked out as well as some of the elements. The designer explored many variations and took into consideration the variety of applications the logo would have.

Once a comfortable combination of elements was chosen the type was designed from scratch, and the final logo was produced.

Designer: Mike Leidel, Atlanta, Georgia
Client: John H. Harland Company

This project was to develop a logo that would graphically represent the name and service of the individual, as well as maintain professionalism.

Rough ideas

Combining the letter and symbol

Simplifying the "G"

Alternate idea

Designer: LeeAnn Brook, Nevada City, California
Client: Ron Greene, Clinical Psychologist

Client is a Boston based product and industrial photo group. When
deciding on a mark we chose to use two elements.

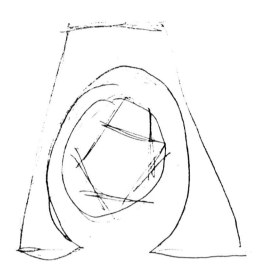
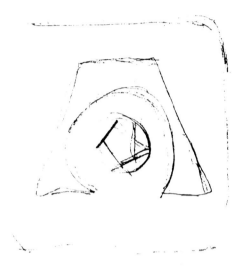

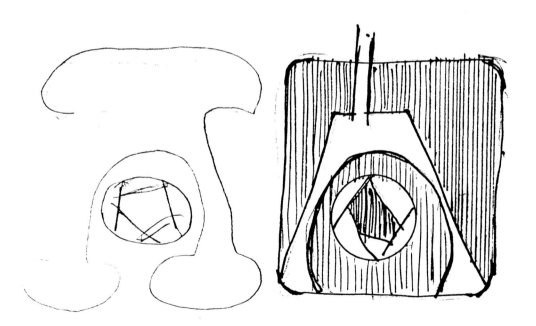

The first was a type element and the second, some design element from within the camera.

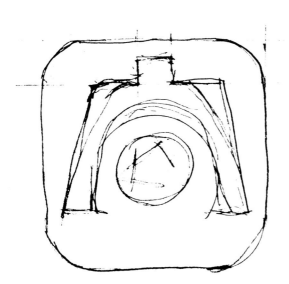
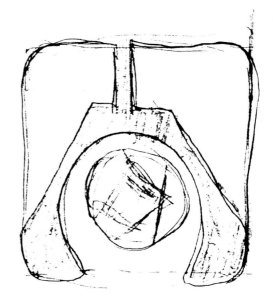

After several attempts to have the mark contained within some geometric shape, with no success, we decided to have the mark stand on its own.

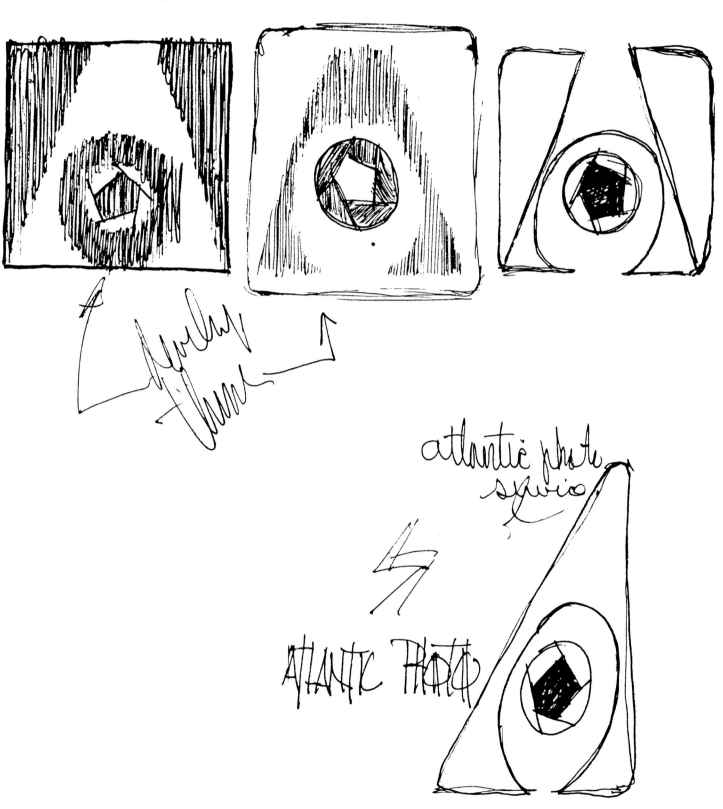

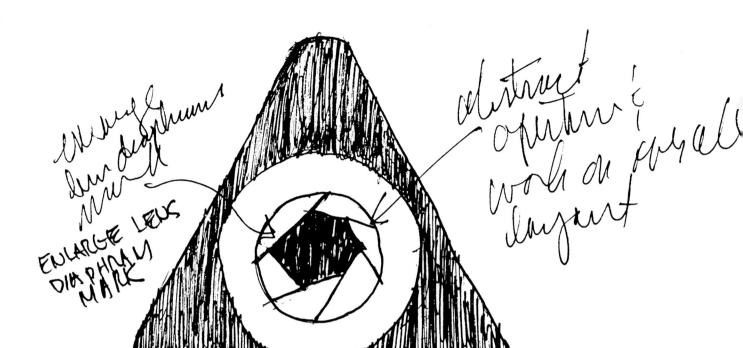

enlarge lens diaphragm mark

ENLARGE LENS
DIAPHRAM
MARK

abstract
aperture &
work on overall
layout

ABSTRACT APERTURE RING &
WORK ON OVERALL LAYOUT.

ATLANTIC
PHOTO
~~SERVICE~~

ATLANTIC PHOTO GROUP

The mark was then designed on the heavy side to convey the feeling of strength and dependability and at the same time project the contemporary attitude of the group.

The type element became a very stylish modern letter "A" supporting an abstracted lens diagram.

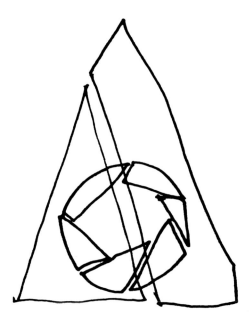

The mark accomplished our plan of having the group identified by its mark independent of its name or any type elements.

Designer: Ciro Giordano, Boston/Wakefield, Massachusetts
Client: Atlantic Photo Group

Our point of departure was Roto-Rooter's existing logo/mark.

In the early stages of design exploration, little is rejected, and one commits to paper most any idea, no matter how trite. One never know where the final solution will come from.

Although management recognized the mark's visual liabilities, they were at first reluctant to abandon it totally. Therefore, we were asked to investigate a broad spectrum of possibilities, ranging from a solution more or less reminiscent of the old mark to a completely new one.

Hence our efforts at depicting a cross-section of pipe containing water even though that message was rarely understood by the general public or even by the people within the company.

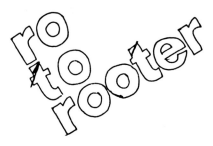

In addition to pictoral symbols, we explored purely typographic directions. While it is usually difficult to recall or retrace the steps in the design process, it is obvious, in this case, that the final solution grew out of the overlapping O's. By the time we arrived here, it became simply a mechanical problem of translating a halftone sketch into line.

What had started as a purely typographic solution took on symbolic meaning as well with the "snake" expressing the nature of Roto-Rooter's basic service of cleaning drains and sewers.

Finally, and probably most important, the mark has the flexibility of being contained in the signature, combining trademark and logotype into one single element, or of being used independently when space limitations or emphasis demand that treatment.

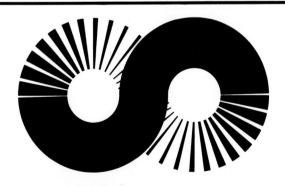

ROTO·ROOTER

Designer: George Tscherny, Inc., New York, New York
Client: Roto-Rooter Corporation

I was chosen to design the Gill Group because I had designed the logo for the Kim Dawson Agency.

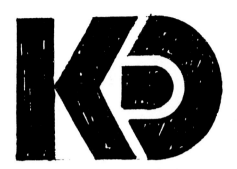 

THE GROUP

THE GILL GROUP

THE GILL GROUP

There was a need to maintain a family look for this affiliate of the Kim Dawson Modeling Agency.

The Gill Group functions as a talent agency for actors.

Designer: Nash Hernandez, Dallas, Texas
Client: The Gill Group

Goffstein, Gaston & Nakash is a company devoted to real estate and construction projects for investment purposes. The company was originally called "Double G" when it only had two partners.

The double G with the plus sign was based on the inherent characteristic of the letter "G," but it did not meet the design criteria even though the designer was encouraged with its development.

Again, the inherent structural characteristics of the letter "G" came into play as the final selection.

The client wanted a symbol to refect a "clean" image that showed precision and regularity. The goal was to devise a symmetrical trademark that gave equal importance to all three partners through the use of their initials.

In order to give a more definitive shape to the symbol a curvilinear border was fitted around the connected letters. The client agreed to the final variation.

Designer: Allan Miller, San Diego, California
Client: Goffstein, Gaston & Nakash

121

The client wanted a house involved in the logo to achieve the visual impact of her realty business.

Since this approach has been repeated many times before, I also included an initial design, which she eventually used.

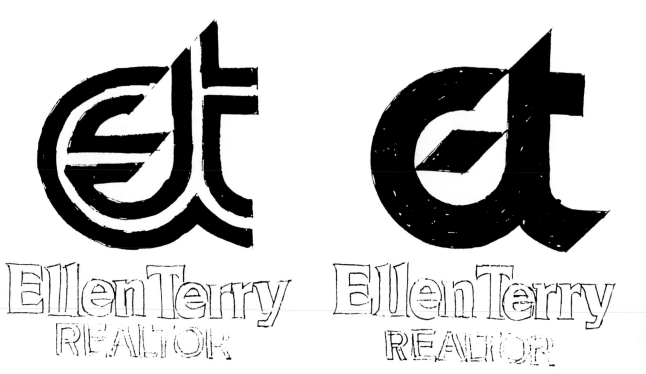

Designer: Nash Hernandez, Dallas, Texas
Client: Ellen Terry Realtor

The Stevens Group has become the stockholding company for the Dial Agency. They function as a professional placement agency for people with college degrees. The "S" is designed to achieve a plural or group feeling.

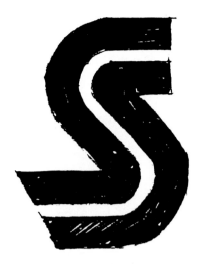

The St..phens Group

The Stephens Group

Designer: Nash Hernandez, Dallas, Texas
Client: The Stevens Group

Nicholas & Dial Agency is a professional Employment Agency for individuals with college degrees. The assignment was to design a logo for an employment agency catering to professional clients. This is why I incorporated the attache case in the design.

Designer: Nash Hernandez, Dallas, Texas
Client: Nicholas & Dial Agency

This is a printing company dealing with four-color processes. My first approach was to depict the rollers used in the printing process and incorporate them in the initial "R" design. The four-color bar guide found on proof sheets gave me the idea to use these colors in designing the corporate mark.

Designer: Nash Hernandez, Dallas, Texas
Client: Rhea Printing Company

This project was to develop a name recognition and service.

Rough sketch of a water faucet

Graphic development of water

Graphic development of water and faucet

Combining the type and graphics

Designer: LeeAnn Brook, Nevada City, California
Client: Sierra Water Systems

Albuquerque National Bank wanted a corporate logo. They indicated they would like an "A" shape, which is what the designer started with.

Revolving the shape produced a symmetrical symbol that had an "indian" and "mountain" look that, in the designer's opinion, helped to suggest the bank's locale. The designer was satisfied with the overall shape, but still had to refine and simplify.

Designer: Debbie McKinney, John H. Harland Co., Albuquerque, Mexico

Client: Albuquerque National Bank

Potter/Wynn, Inc. wanted a logo showing both initials unified in one corporate identity.

POTTER/WYNNE

POTTER/WYNNE

POTTER/WYNNE

POTTER/WYNNE

The client demanded a Texas image with aviation in mind because of his aviation clientele.

POTTER/WYNNE

POTTER/WYNNE

Designer: Nash Hernandez, Dallas, Texas
Client: Potter/Wynne, Inc.

131

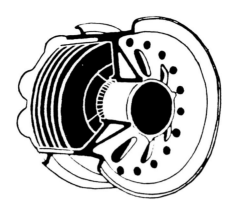

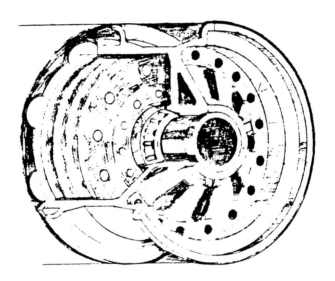

When we were approached by the B.F. Goodrich Company for suggestions on a logo for their aircraft wheel and brake division, they told us that the mark must be based on a cross section of a brake for the space shuttle. They provided this drawing and a photograph of the actual brake.

Our first step was to do a rendering to get the feel for what the brake looked like. The drawing flattened out the perspective to produce a more symbol-like mark.

Our next step was to produce a series of roughs to explore the method of indicating motion coming to a halt.

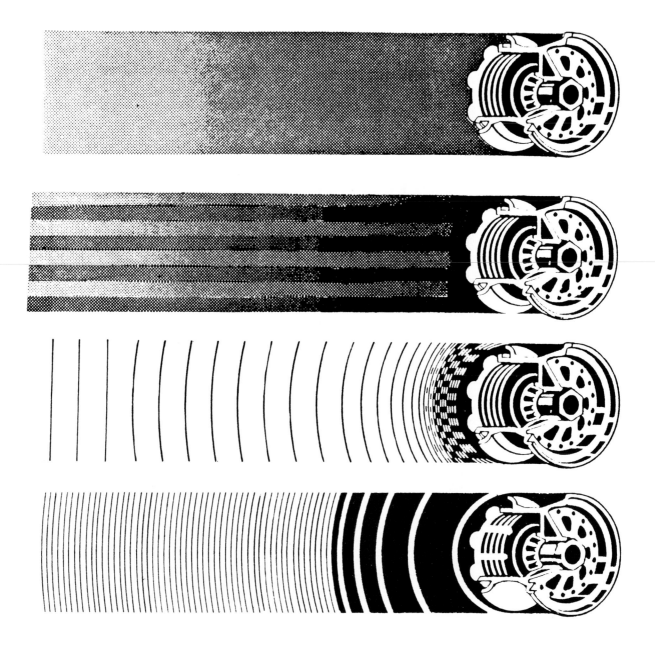

We felt that the best way to show this was to indicate motions by a series of thin vertical lines, and the slowing and stopping of that motion by the gradual progression of the thin lines to thick lines and finally to black.

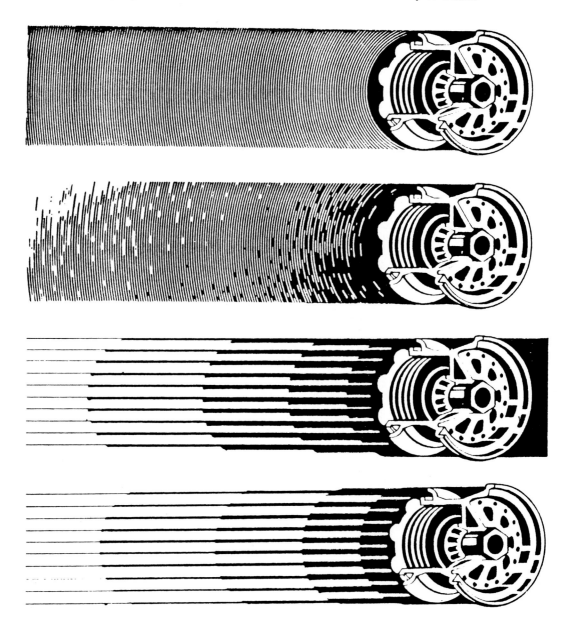

Also, alternate line motion studies were considered.

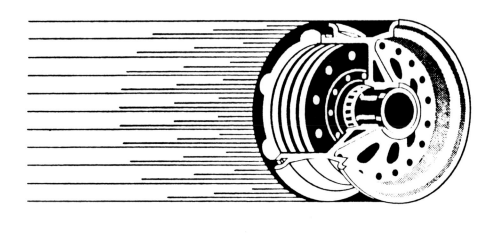

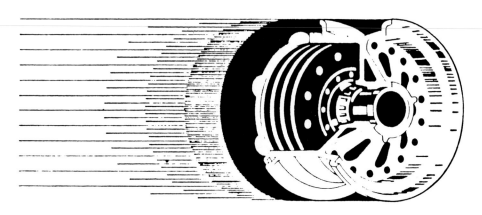

A few more studies were made on the brake drawing concentrating on the best way to render the curved white surface of the rim.

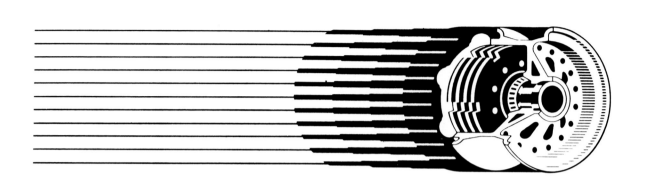

BFGoodrich

The BFGoodrich Company
Transportation Products Division

P.O. Box 340
Troy, Ohio 45373

**Aircraft
Wheels &
Brakes**

The final logo.

The finished logo as used with type and the B. F. Goodrich corporate identifier.

Designer: Walter M. Herip Design Associates, Hudson, Ohio
Client: The B.F. Goodrich Company

charlotte's web

Charlotte's Web

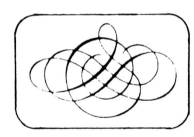

When we were first approached to design the mark for Charlotte's Web, a card and gift shop, we were asked to avoid using a spider's web because of its connotations of fear.

In the first example, we chose to use the definition of web that relates to woven cloth.

In the second example, the possibility of using a delicate web-like ornament was explored.

Both thumbnails were shown to the client before going any further, in an effort not to spend too much time on the project.

After seeing the first two roughs, the client liked the type form of the second example. However, she reconsidered the use of a spider's web. She asked us to explore the possibility of using a web in combination with a flower.

The final layout rough as shown to the client.

Charlotte's Web

The finished art differed only in the size of the flower on the mark.

Charlotte's Web

Designer: Walter M. Herip Design Associates, Hudson, Ohio
Client: Charlotte's Web

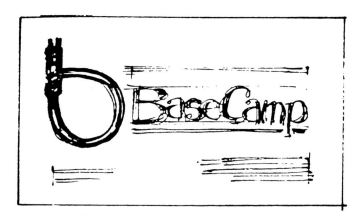

Base Camp is a retail outfitter of outdoor sports equipment. Our only limitiation was that the name should be part of the logo.

We did some roughs and came up with a typeface that had the strength and boldness to suggest the outdoor, rugged feeling we were trying to portray.

We felt that a rope was a basic tool used in camping, climbing, canoeing and other outdoor adventure sports. It was the common denominator that we were looking for.

However, when we combined the image of the knot with the typeface, they seemed seperate and didn't work together as a whole. So we began to incorporate the knot of the rope into the type. It helped pull the design together, but the overall appearance still needed to be resolved.

141

We experimented with the spacing of the characters and found that by dropping down the "C," the top of the word formed a good "base" for the logo. But we still weren't satisfied with the rope. The final design is a mark that has the rugged, outdoor look we were after.

Designer: Walter M. Herip Design Associates, Hudson, Ohio
Client: Base Camp

The objective of the Calusa Cove identification project was to develop a logo expressive of the life style offered by a unique seaside development.

Calusa Cove is a natural harbor located in the Fort Myers, Florida area.

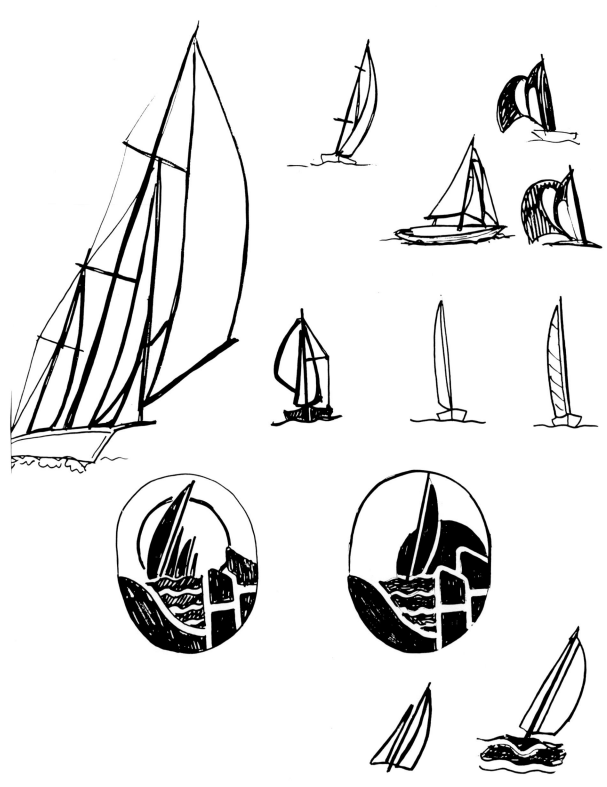

Logo development was somewhat difficult due to the many graphic elements required to communicate a "harbor" concept.

None the less, an elegant and strong symbol was the final result.

Designer: Babcock & Schmid Inc., Bath, Ohio
Client: Calusa Cove

WBBS-TV, Channel 60 in Chicago, retained my services to design an I.D. logo for their newly established channel.

I began my rough idea by creating symbols which would be associated with television work.

The client was not enthusiastic about this because he felt that the number 60 had to be a predominant element in the design.

Several roughs were created with this new concept but any of these could be identified with any channel 60 in any other state.

Finally, I decided to add the Sears Tower building (where the station is located) to identify the channel with the city. The idea worked and the client was pleased.

WBBS-TV•CHANNEL 60

Designer: Silvio Gayton, Miami, Florida
Client: WBBS-TV — Channel 60, Chicago, Illinois

The Port of Anchorage, Alaska, retained T.H. Reynolds Advertising to design a logo image that would help define the port as a seperate entity from the local municipal government operations. We were given free "unlimited" reign to come up with a strong representational graphic that would have international appeal.

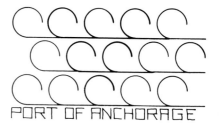

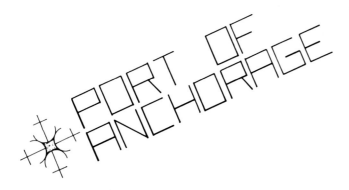

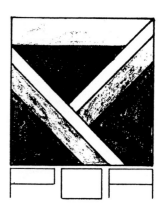

Various general symbols were discussed such as ships, loading cranes, anchors, stars and waves. The logo design would have to be adaptable to a variety of useages, from lapel pins to building graphics.

PORT OF ANCHORAGE

PORT OF ANCHORAGE

PORT OF ANCHORAGE

149

PORT OF ANCHORAGE

PORT OF ANCHORAGE

150

A series of roughs were presented for initial screening, by the port selection committee, to narrow the designing efforts. A wide range of styles was submitted by the department artists, from bold letter application to intricate color design to graphic symbolism. The committee narrowed the selection to a series of 4 anchors in a snowflake design, a single anchor within a snowflake and a series of 3 overlapping anchors.

The overlapping anchors was finally chosen. The colors were deep blue for the anchors and a deep red for the lettering with a black outline when applicable.

The anchors provided 3 representational designs: an obvious nautical association, the upper portion represents the working cooperation between people and an overall abstract of an early sailing vessel.

PORT OF ANCHORAGE

Kabel typeface was selected for its bold, strong face, which has a serif edge similar to those found on the anchors.

Designer: Thomas H. Reynolds, Anchorage, Alaska
Client: The Port of Anchorage

As a designer and a fine artist I tend to work with solid shapes and thought my logo should reflect that.

I began with the initials P.D.S. (Pattinian Design Studio) and worked with that for a while.

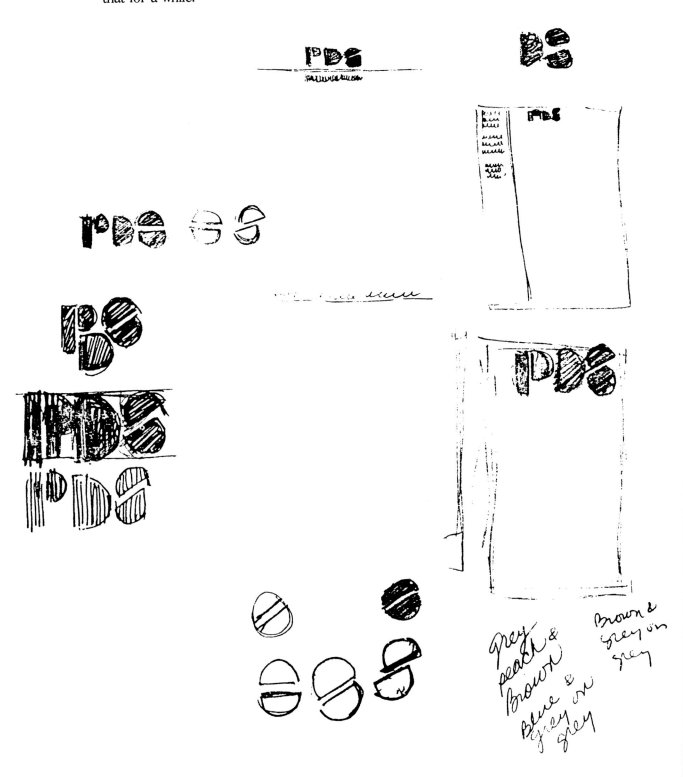

I wanted to get some movement into the design and started breaking apart
the logo, having it floating freely on the page.

Feeling this wasn't working, I then thought of just using the circle, square and triangle to represent the basic elements of design. I began using these elements in a series whereby they started out overlapping each other and then moved apart to the individual shapes.

It seemed to be too much and, ultimately, I just settled on the first design of the series and used that as my logo.

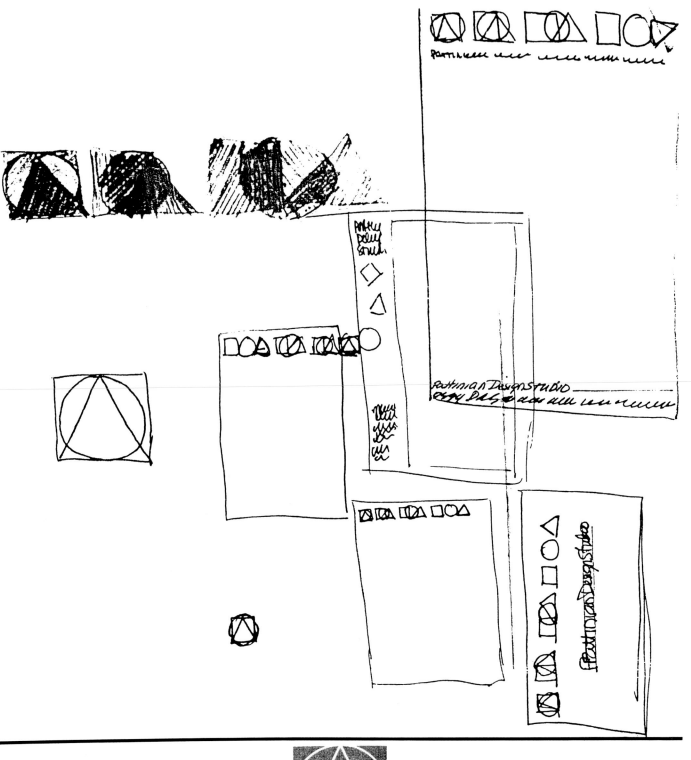

Designer: Merri Mechanick-Pattinian, San Diego, California
Client: Pattinian Design Studio

Airlift Northwest is an airplane medical transportation service sponsored by four hospitals. Each hospital is specialized in treating heart, children, burn and cancer.

The logo was not to favor any one hospital. The clients' main request was that the logo had to have a very "professional look." And it is not an emergency service but an informal and friendly "loving-care" service.

I presented three designs in the following sequence:

First, the idea with a heart and wings excited the hospital that specialized in heart treatment but the others rejected quickly.

Second, and my least favorite design, was an attempt to blend the "professional look" with "friendly look".

Finally, I presented my favorite design.

Four square dots in red symbolize four hospitals, while the negative space forms the medical symbol. The type treatment is not new but appropriate.

AIRLIFT ▪▪
NORTHWEST

Designer: Gene Davis & Associates, Seattle, Washington
Client: Airlift Northwest

We were called in to redesign an existing logo for a Shirtmaker Company. The client wanted the logo updated. Our client also stressed that the logo type should be clean and simple and suggested overlapping her name with the manufacturer's name.

We worked up a series of roughs. From these we selected three ideas to present to the client—one idea following the client's direction and two alternate ideas.

158

We presented our three ideas in a pretty tight format, even giving some tentative color suggestions. We felt the ideas gave the client a chance to visualize her suggestions and to see some alternate directions. The two alternate ideas also lend themselves to using part of the logo as a symbol, i.e.: for appliques to the shirts themselves either on the pocket or cuff, or as a trademark in future advertising and promotion. The client was happy with all three ideas and took them to review with her associates.

Combining the initials "B" and "W" to create a shirtcollar with bow tie lending possibilites for this to be used as a symbol.

Using the two "B's" from Bonnie and Balfour to create a logo symbol.

At our next meeting with the client, the final selection was made. After consulting with her associates, the client felt that the two alternate ideas did not suit her market. The "B" logo, which everyone really liked, was considered too chic. The logo with the "BW" creating a shirt collar with a bow tie was perceived as too tricky.

Therefore everyone agreed and liked the simpler logo design, following the client's original directions. We then took this logo and made some refinements working with size, caps vs. lower case and weights, also experimenting with overlapping the letters in the manufacturer's name. Color decisions were also made at this time for the inside of the outline type.

The final logo — using bold type for both shirtmakers and the designer's name gave better balance and more impact to the logo in the market place. The outline type was filled in with a bright blue. The final application will be for shirt labels, hangtags and stationery.

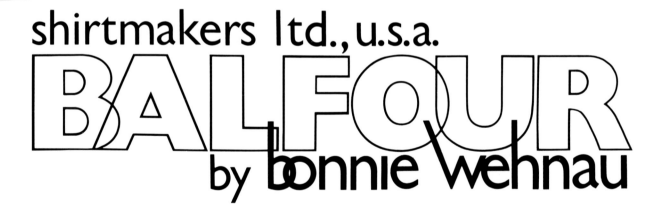

Designer: Adrienne Y. Carlin, AYC Graphics, New York, New York
Client: Balfour Shirtmakers Ltd., New York, New York

Gordon H. Dickinson, a private financial consultant, enjoyed an excellent reputation among his clients but had never tried to expand his business by conveying his sophisticated services through his business printed materials.

Because of the range of financial services offered, a single symbol did not seem feasible in the beginning series of roughs, and emphasis was soon placed on the full name or initials GHD, since the business was dependent upon one individual.

 A line version of the initials and the name set to match type on U.S. currency emerged as two solid possibilities.

GORDON DICKINSON

The nagging feeling persisted, however, that a more clear cut way of expressing the business existed. Early doodles of math symbols were reexamined. All four simple math signs were actually present in the combination multiplication/division signs. This simple solution seemed appropriate for one who found ways to make money grow.

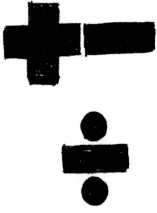 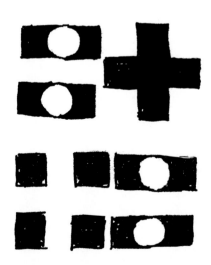 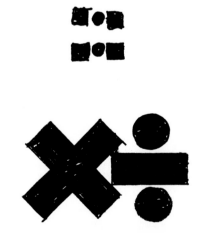

A sans serif face combined with the symbol seemed to cold.

A face with more personality plus the informality of lower case was a perfect counter to the geometric symbol.

The client was extremely pleased with the final combination of symbol and logotype.

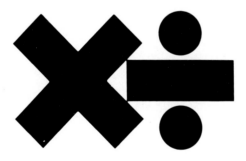

Designer: David and Nora Bullock, Kutztown, Pennsylvania
Client: Gordon H. Dickinson

The Library of Congress called me in to work on a logo project for "A National Preservation Program Publication." The program publishes books and leaflets discussing how to preserve the printed page — book, newspapers, etc. The Library had no idea or direction they wanted to follow. After talking to the proper people, gathering facts, I returned with the following designs.

The Library choose the three "p's" protected by the "N". I thought the answer to the visual problem was the hands, visually discribing human protection of valued books.

They accepted the lower case "n" protecting the three "p's" in a decorative style. The logo will be printed on all of their title pages or cover 4 of their books and leaflets.

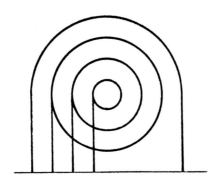

A National Preservation Program Publication

Designer: Pat Taylor, Washington, D.C.
Client: Library of Congress, "A National Preservation Program Publication"

ADMSA is an acronym that signifies Arquitectura de Desarrollos Maritimos, S.A. This Mexican architectural firm specializes in planning and designing marinas and coastal properties.

The basic visual direction was dictated by the subject and geographic locations of the company's operations. Thus, tropical plants, sun, weather phenomena and nautical themes were top priority. Also, the letter "A" was a direction that the client considered as a viable direction.

Some experimentation was undertaken with the exclusive use of letters to form acronyms, but these efforts were unsatisfactory to the artist.

The eventual solution embodied the abstract form of sail boats and the letter "A".

The client was pleased with the solution because it reflected a "fresh" look that related to the ocean and cheerful, vibrant characteristics of the sites in which the developments were located.

Designer: Allan Miller, San Diego, California
Client: ADMSA

167

FEBCA is an international trade center located in Tijuana and Baja. The center has exposition halls and goods available for sale and inspection. Feria de Baja California is the name of the company, which is reduced to the acronym FEBCA.

Since many of the products featured at FEBCA come from the orient, it was thought that some indication of the east might be included in the design of the trademark. However, as the trademark developed, it became apparent the symbolic treatment alone would not evoke enough recognition in this particular case. Thus, a logo was developed to work in tandem with the trademark.

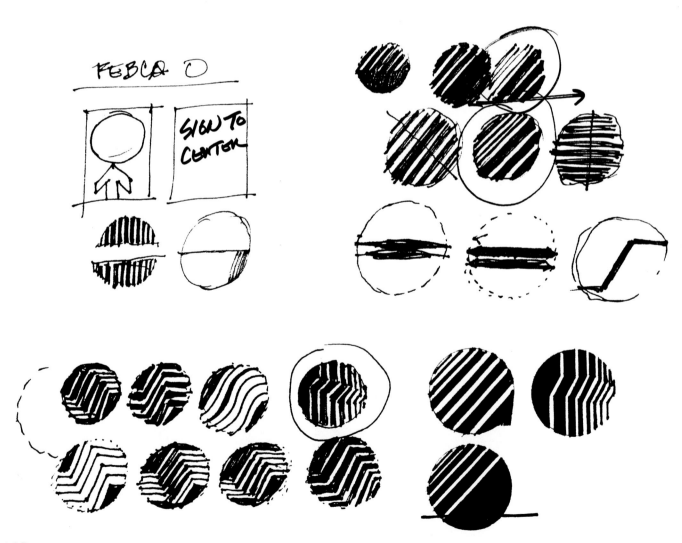

A tight time limit was a deciding factor so the "rising sun" idea and the sun moving across the horizon remained as the central theme. Also, street signs showing the way to the FEBCA Center were needed, therefore, the combination of logo and trademark was intended to accomodate a directional arrow underneath the grouping of symbols.

Designer: Allan Miller, San Diego, California
Client: FEBCA

The city of Tijuana annually records the most numerous entries of tourists of any city in the world. It is a city that unofficially has over one-million inhabitants. Additionally, it is designated as a free trade zone by the Mexican government, thus, it is particularly attractive to American and other foreign tourists. The Comite de Turismo y Convenciones de Tijuana, the Tijuana Tourism & Convention Bureau, decided that the numerous tourists needed endorsements of stores, directional graphics, information booths and the feeling that a citizen to citizen committee existed to give assistance.

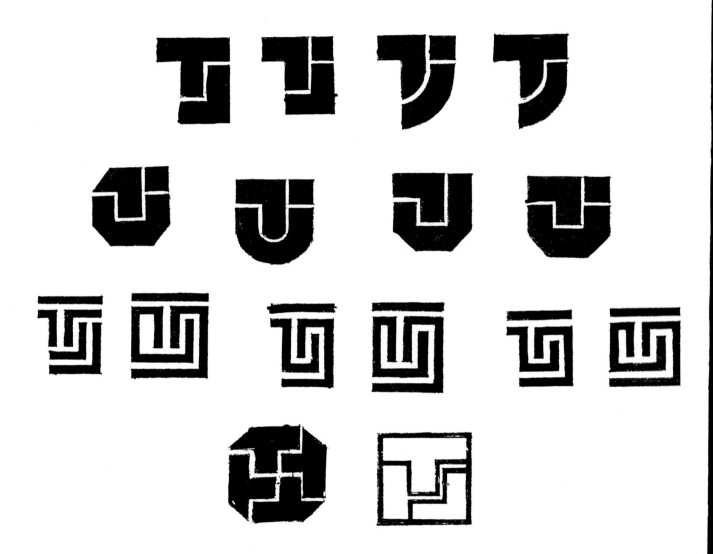

The Americans who live near the border informally refer to Tijuana as "T.J." While this is not a favorite acknowledgement by the Mexicans, it was felt by the client and the Mexican Advertising Agency handling the account that this was an acceptable if not favored approach for the sake of name recognition. Thus, all the preliminary development featured this approach.

Since the artist was familiar with Mexican Pre-Columbian visual treatments, these motifs were manifested in character throughout the sketches, both consciously and perhaps subconsciously. The agency endorses this manifestation although it was not overly encouraged since Mexican Pre-Columbian tribes did not inhabit the area as was the case in Central Mexico. In fact, the city of Tijuana is about ninety-two years old.

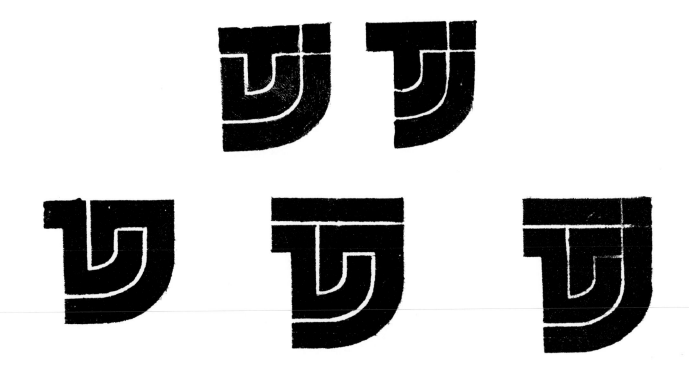

The trademark had to be a simplified form because it was to be applied to many items, i.e. signs, window decals, printed matter, newspaper ads, etc. Therefore, a bold design was favored with rather thick design members. The design was conceived to be in two colors occasionally, so none of the members touch each other. This makes the preparation of camera ready art work easy.

Designer: Allan Miller, Tijuana, B.C. Mexico
Client: Tijuana Tourism & Convention Bureau

171

My task was to design a logo which would be a 3 dimensional, full-color sign.

My first sketches toyed with various typefaces and symbols—the nervous father, the happy doctor, etc.

The large round "O's" of this sketch seemed to have the most possibilities.

I liked it so far, and so did the client, but wanted something from the "pink and blue" world of babies. To solve this I went back to an idea from the first sketches: add a figure — babies, doctors, fathers, anything that had to do with birth and reproduction. Humorously, the rabbit suggested itself. I remembered a line from a children's book — "I'm late, I'm late . . ." And so it jelled. I used a rabbit, dressed in a waistcoat to give him watch-pocket, and therefore a watch.

172

I now placed the rabbit — looking at his watch — *outside* the word "room". I think it worked.

I had to create a round bottom; therefore added "the square" for balance.

Then I added the textured screen to set off the white rabbit. Then, finally, total screens were decided upon to create the 3 dimensional effect that the original sign had.

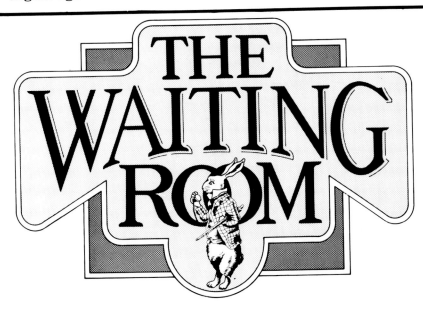

Designer: Tom Ambrosino, Neversink, New York
Client: The Waiting Room, Liberty, New York

Marika is a company that produces dance and exercise wear comparable in style to that of Danskin. Since it is produced in the Orient, it is available at a greatly reduced price.

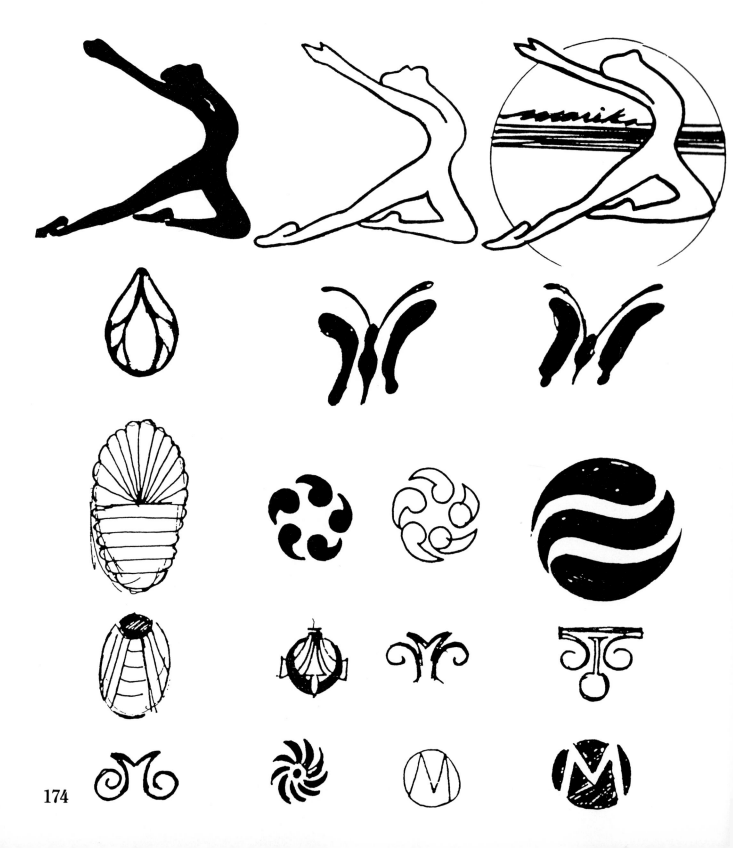

I pursued several different directions trying to design a mark that could be used for all of their printed material as well as being embroidered onto the garments themselves.

After much effort we decided a hand lettered script would act as their logotype with a small red heart dropped off to the right as their mark.

Marikā *lectura*

♥MARIKA *squiria*

marika *camellia*

MARIKA *optima*

marika *cirkulus*

marika *cut-in-fold*

MARIKA *fimo*

marika

marika

Marika *gallio*

MARIKA *premier eightline*

MARIKA

All garments would have a red heart embroidered on, positioned approximately at the hip bone.

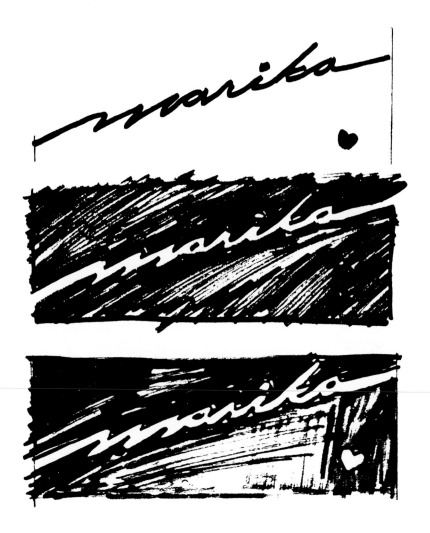

Designer: Pattinian Design Studio, San Diego, California
Client: Marika

Seafood Sally's is a fish and chips fast food restaurant.

The assignment was to depict a family oriented, fun place to eat at a neighborhood mall.

Designer: Nash Hernandez, Dallas, Texas
Client: Seafood Sally's

Carpet Tree

Carpet Tree

The design for Carpet Tree depicts the end of a carpet roll, unifying the tree as a corporate symbol.

Carpet Tree

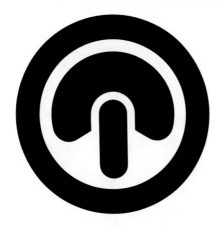

Designer: Nash Hernandez, Dallas, Texas
Client: Carpet Tree

The Jolly Ox Club is a night club located inside the Steak and Ale Restaurants.

It was necessary to maintain the English Pub look.

Designer: Nash Hernandez, Dallas, Texas
Client: Jolly Ox Club

Our client wanted a logo that would be contemporary and, at the same time, reflect a feeling of holiday warmth and tradition.

From the inception of this project, we felt using a symbol representing Christmas and the holidays was necessary in addition to the name itself.

We submitted several graphic approaches, but the client felt they lacked the warmth that she wanted to project.

So, trying a more "calligraphic" approach, we submitted a rough design incorporating an ornament. We altered the typestyle used on the name and wrapped the words around the symbol. This made it work as one unit.

The logo, a graphic, straight-edged ornament working with a softer, Serif typeface, was exactly the desired approach, projecting the good feelings of Christmas, necessary for a store involved soley in holiday merchandise.

Designer: Tissa Porter Advertising, Bryan, Texas
Client: The Christmas Store

185

Bud Wertheim—artist, sculptor, and puppeteer—wanted a logo for his puppet theatre and insisted that the word "unstrung" be prominent. Because he is well-known in the area, my first roughs looked at the possibilities in his name. Nothing suggested itself, and I focused on "unstrung." To emphasize "unstrung," I used a large serif typeface, and gave "puppet theater" a smaller, carnival-type look.

I liked the basic idea but thought it too short and wide. I decided to add Bud's name to the top to give it height.

At this stage it struck me that the arch supporting "unstrung" could be seen as the proscenium arch of the stage . . . I put people on stage. The idea came to use a puppet here.

This was the first design I showed the client. He was pleased generally, liked the "stage" idea very much and wanted to accent it. He gave me his own pen-and-ink that he wanted to use, a sketch of Punch and Judy, which is one of his more famous productions.

I felt it was too busy and detailed for the existing logo and would fight with my typefaces. I asked if we could compromise. We could. In a book of designs in the public domain I found a picture from *Punch* magazine.

I drew a pen and ink version of the puppet. I increased the size of the stage opening. I decided to give the puppet an "impish look" and gave him scissors — to cut the strings. I now had "unstrung" prominent. I had the puppet he wanted. And the scissors in the hand of the puppet conveyed the idea of "unstrung."

Designer: Tom Ambrosino, Neversink, New York
Client: Bud Wertheim "The Unstrung Puppet Theatre," Livingston Manor, New York

This project was a signage program for the largest metropolis in the two Carolinas.

In order to give the client a broad view of logo/logotype design for the city, we initially took three different design directions.

International symbol (abstract form) to identify city as a growing, dynamic place.

Symbol derived from the Hornet's Nest, which is an old standing symbol, or mascot, for Mecklenburg County in which Charlotte is located.

Symbol derived from the crown - Charlotte is named after Queen Charlotte of England, and is known as the "Queen City."

After city officials approved the crown direction, we developed and proposed an abstract, contemporary crown.

CITY
OF
CHARLOTTE

After much news media attention throughout the city, both pro and con, the logo was revised and the new crown logo/logotype combination was approved by City Council.

CHARLOTTE

Designer: Joe Sonderman, Charlotte, North Carolina
Client: City of Charlotte, North Carolina

A quality developer in South Carolina retained me to design a logo for a condominium project at Hilton Head Island. The project was to be called Breakers.

The client wanted a design that would be very strong and that would compete with the already graphic Hilton Head market.

Designing a logo is like putting a puzzle together. When all of the pieces are fitted into place, the design is achieved.

I felt this design should have a wave or breaker in it somewhere. Researching waves, I found most were dated and not effective. After many attempts with designing a breaker, I came up with a strong symbol of a wave. I did this in bold lines, enabling me to use it in black & white or multicolors.

The first piece of my puzzle was complete. I dove into the rest of the design. I knew at this point, the symbol, breaker, had to be a part of a total design. By itself it would not hold water, so to speak.

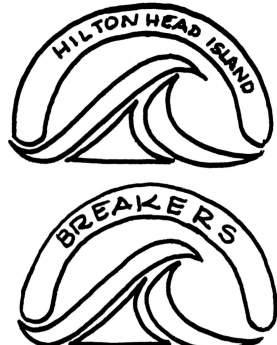

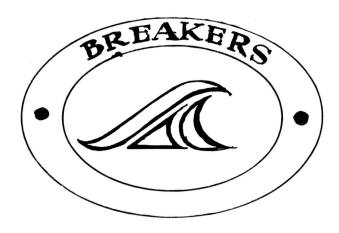

194

After several attempts I knew I was close. The arch around the symbol seemed to be the only solution. The symmetry, the nautical look had been accomplished. With a little more work we decided to incorporate Hilton Head in the design. The arch supplied the area for this, thus allowing me to cap off the bottom of the logo with "Breakers". The design was accomplished. It passed appearance, flexible enough to be used in one color or multi-colors.

After the design was approved, the developer told me of two other projects that he would like to have done. These projects were to have the same appearance as the Breakers. This is how they came out.

Designer: Don Connelly, Avondale est., Georgia
Client: The Breakers

Employee Counseling Programs was a program initiated by the JBFCS-
Jewish Board of Family and Children's Services, whose logo we had designed. The company's aim was to increase productivity in large and small corporations by counseling their employees. The idea behind it was that if
employees have an outlet for their family and health problems, they would
not bring their problems to work and thus their employers would benefit
from better employee relations and higher productivity.

We tried many different directions in our initial presentation. A puzzle was
designed with identical pieces, except for one, or with one puzzle piece that
won't fit in.

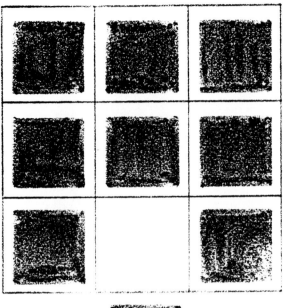

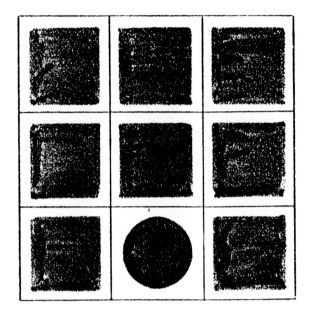

In another solution we used geometrical shapes: triangles, dots, and squares to represent people. In each design there was one odd shape, or a shape outside the frame that did not fit in with the rest. These ideas implied that the program was designed to help those individuals who do not fit in and who feel alienated in their work and environment.

We also used images of the human face to make the logo appear more appealing and humanitarian. In one design, all the faces, but one, face the same direction. In another, the image of the face is broken up, suggesting that the person is not a balanced, happy employee.

Although our clients loved our presentation, they felt that it did not serve their specific needs, which included catering to big corporations. They wanted a simple typographic solution.

We suggested one design using the letters "ECP" and three geometric people figures. This image related to the JBFCS, the parent company's logo.

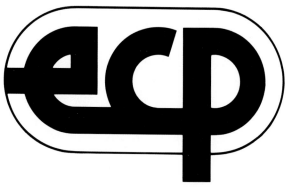

Employee Counseling Programs

In our final solution, we joined the letters "ECP," the initials of the Company's name. The letters were shaped geometrically, but the joining suggested integration and continuity. We liked this image, but felt that it was not quite right, so we added a frame around the whole image. The "E" touches the frame and the "P" extends outside the frame. This image shows that the company extends a helping hand to people with problems but is within the corporate group. We added the full name of the company under the logo to reinforce it.

Designer: Itzhak Berry, New York, New York
Client: Employee Counseling Programs

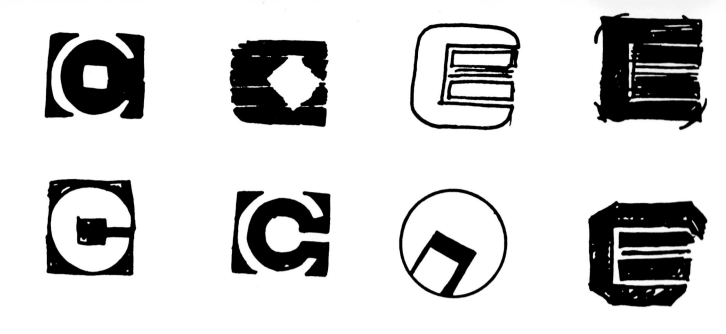

We tried to combine a strong corporate look that could compete with any computer company in the world, including IBM, Sony, etc. This mark had to be so simple and strong that it would indicate the computer store's purpose, yet be graphically recognizable to this particular company.

We tried to combine a "C" with a micro chip, which eventually led to a chip in the middle of the "C." The purpose was to combine a strong corporate "C" with a delicate micro chip.

The typeface used had to be strong enough to work with the logo. Hence, the heavy, condensed type that reflects the feeling of the logo.

CompuMicro Inc. is the parent company of CompuMicro Inc. Computer Store. The two variations show the flexibility of the logo and type.

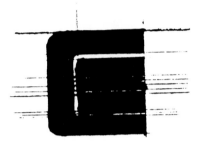

Designer: John Kneapler and Patrick Daugherty
Package/Graphic/Corporate Design
Client: CompuMicro Inc., Staten Island, New York

For this project of an office building development, three directions were submitted to the client. The Helvetica logo, though legible and contemporary, seemed too cold.

greystone

greyStone

Its treatment as pieces of stone was too rustic.

GREYSTONE

Second, the logo in Roman stone cut letters was appreciated for its classical and dignified look, but then considered too traditional for a new building.

Finally the client was seduced by the refined elegance of the script letters. The adopted version, symmetry balanced with two curlicues, has been reinforced with a strong bar of color. This logo gives its seal of quality to a most successful project.

Greystone

Grey Stone

Grey Stone

Greystone

Designer: John Follis & Associates, Los Angeles, California
Client: Greystone

John Follis & Associates' assignment was to develop a symbol, in conjunction with an architectural signing system and wall graphics, for McCarran International Airport in Las Vegas.

The development of a pictogram of an airplane was a natural starting point.

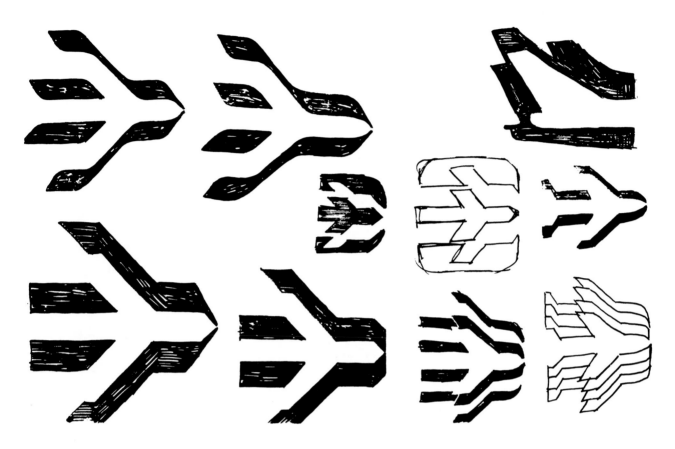

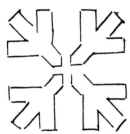

McCARRAN
INTERNATIONAL
AIRPORT

McCARRAN

M CARRAN

The grouping of this element in a pleasing and positive arrangement
resulted in a design that quickly and simply conveys the essence of an international airport.

The symbol suggests a crossroad or meeting place and can effectively be applied to a number of diverse elements from large identification signs to a letterhead.

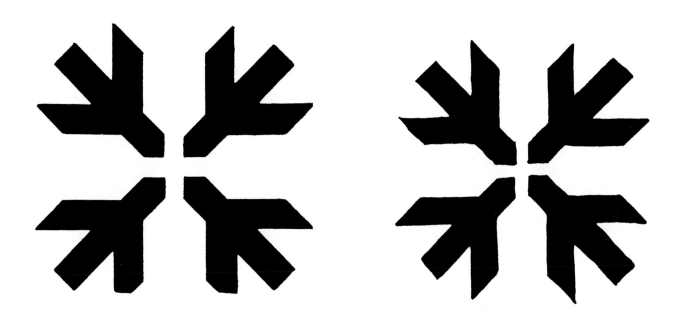

Designer: John Follis & Associates, Los Angeles, California
Client: McCarran International Airport

We were retained by the "Region 3 Soaring Association" to develop a mark
to be used on stationery, window stickers, shoulder patches, etc.

We began with stylized sketches of a bird in flight, but found them awkward when incorporating "Region 3."

We investigated sketches incorporating a soaring plane, mountains, clouds, etc.

Final 3 color version submitted and selected.

Designer: Don Romanelli, Clinton, New York
Client: Region 3 Soaring Association

Expo is a production company for cultural events. It is an American-Israeli service, so its connections are mostly with Israelis and Jews.

They commissioned us to design a logo that would be both modern and easy to remember.

The direction we took was that of a logo-type, working on the shape and balance of the letters in simple geometrical forms. In one of our initial roughs we introduced the Jewish image of a Menorah using circles and straight lines only. But the client was not too enthusiastic.

Our final design is based on circles. The letters "E," "X," and "P" are joined, showing the simple, easy interaction of people in cultural and social events.

Designer: Itzhak Berry, New York, New York
Client: American Israeli Expo Service

This project included the total exhibit, interior and graphic design, including image program/logo for a major new museum of science and technology.

DISCOVERY

DISCOVERY PLACE

DISCOVERY PLACE

DISCOVERY PLACE

The initial image of Discovery Place was considered as an interim logotype to assist the museum with expediting the production of various fund raising packages. Primary emphasis was not directed toward a logo.

After the interim logotype was used for pre-opening museum promotion,

it became apparent that an identifiable symbol reflecting an image of
science and technology would be more successful after opening.

The first stage was to search through existing symbols used in chemistry, physics and other scientific fields.

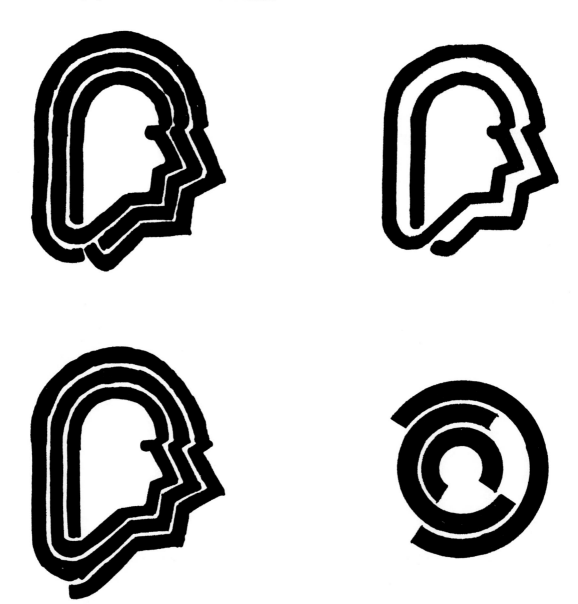

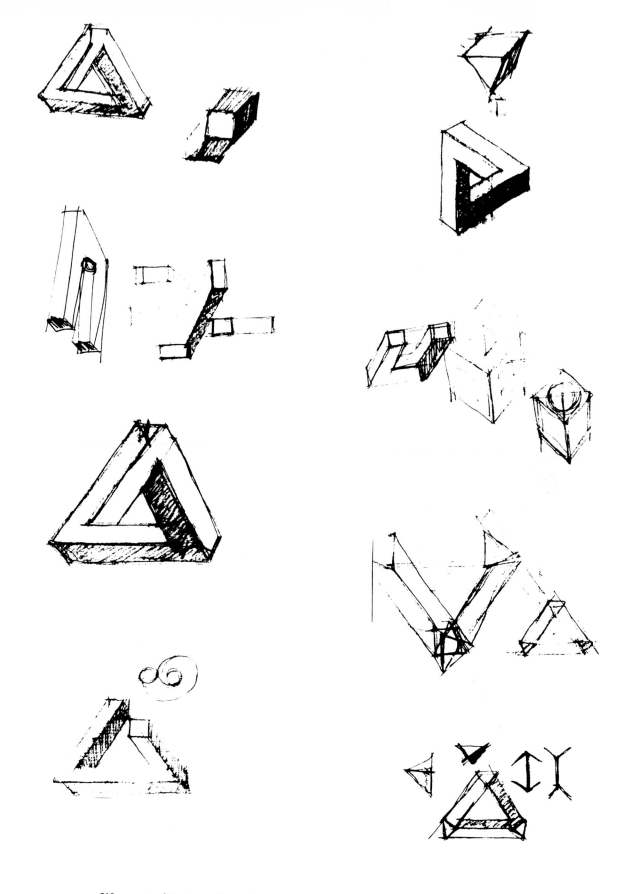

We wanted to translate them into more readable and reproducable forms.

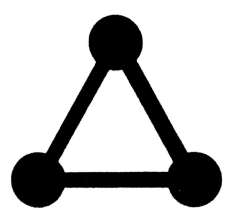

During this process, we came across the "Impossible triangle," which we had used earlier in a three-dimensional visual perception exhibit for the museum.

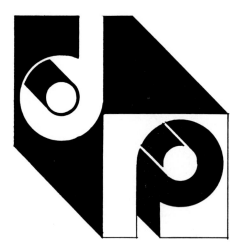

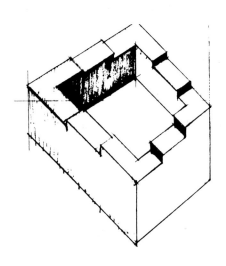

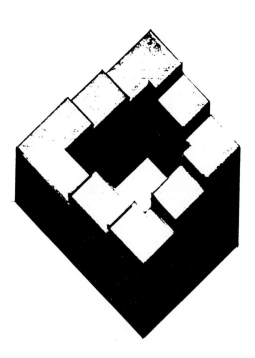

The impossible triangle logo was found to be scientific, dynamic, multidimensional in appearance.

It was found to evoke a sense of wonder from the viewer—a quality also present within the museum itself.

The impossible triangle concept was developed and refined into an ultimate logo that could be reproduced in black-and-white or three colors.

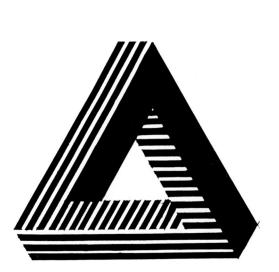

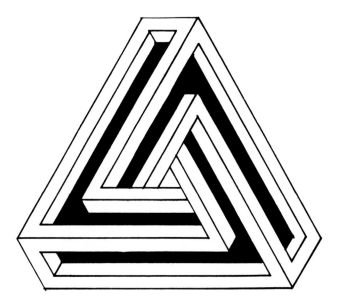

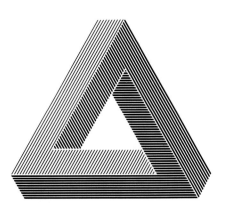

Designer: Joe Sonderman, Charlotte, North Carolina
Client: Science Museums of Charlotte, Inc.

The Sentry Hardware Company's logo was, in part, a literal "minuteman." An identical minuteman was also used by the Continental Insurance Company. In Sentry's case, the minuteman was backed by a U.S. map, several slogans, and surrounded by an early American sign plaque.

Our goal was to modernize the Sentry and continue to use it, due to strong existing recognition.

Additionally, Sentry had a relatively unique position in the industry: A name concept that could be expressed graphically (vs. "True Value," "Ace," and "HWI").

The new Sentry logo creates a dramatic change, is high in impact and of strong retention value.

It has been successfully applied throughout Sentry's 4,500-plus dealer network.

Designer: Babcock & Schmid Associates, Inc., Bath, Ohio
Client: Sentry Hardware Company

While trying to reach clients in the medical profession, we contacted a medical writer and together established a new company.

We called the company Image & Information. The medical writer would supply the information and we would apply the images. Our company aimed to serve hospitals, medical institutions and other medical establishments.

One of our first ideas resembled a yellow pad, with the name Image & Information hand written, spelling out the name of the company.
Another idea was to write the two words in the same helvetica typeface, but make one an outline and the other solid, thus showing that the two different functions of the company are integrated. We wanted to give this logo an advanced, futuristic look to suggest computer-age design for computer-age science.

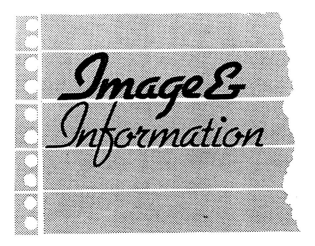

In our final solution we took advantage of the symmetry of the two initials of the company's name. The two "I's" by the "&" show that they are mutually dependent functions incorporated in one company. The use of clean, modern, outlined letters suggests that the company is part of the advanced computer-age.

Designer: Itzhak Berry, New York, New York
Client: Image & Information Co.

Isram Travel Agency retained us to design a logo for their new 2 Million Dollars travel insurance plan. They wanted the design to be conservative and to reflect security and protection.

Our initial roughs used the motifs of sheild, key, seal, lion and eagle to project these ideas of security and protection.

Most of our client's business deals with Mediterranean travel, and they liked the idea of the two columns, which are symbols of the Greek culture and stand for the sum of two million dollars.

We changed the columns' form into a more traditional Greek shape to retain the Mediterranean feeling, and we chose a conservative typeface that we thought suitable for the ancient cultures of the Mediterranean countries and for our client's image.

Designer: Itazhak Berry, New York, New York
Client: Isram Travel

The Butcher, The Baker, The Candlestick Maker is a small European style shopping village of specialized merchants featuring products for the home.

The developer retained John Follis & Associates to create a symbol for the center to be used on a number of items, including a sales brochure and signing elements. The strong theme and descriptive name led us towards a literal yet stylized interpretation of the title.

Our first directions resulted in decorative designs inspired by European woodcuts with trade themes. Some of our initial designs, directly inspired by the poem from which the title is derived, show the three men in the tub. Later, we used only one of the three elements—a candle, a cow, or a shaft of wheat—or some combination of the three elements.

The most successful direction was the stylized drawing of the three characters combined with the logotype in a capsule shape below the image. The full color airbrush version of the final symbol gave a three dimensional quality to the flat areas in the black and white version.

Designer: John Follis & Associates, Los Angeles, California
Client: The Butcher, The Baker, The Candlestick Maker

Cambridge Oil was a new company also involved in security funds. They contracted us to design their logo, which they wanted to project stability and reliability.

We began with two approaches. In one, we used a logotype with a modern typeface to suggest vitality and strength.

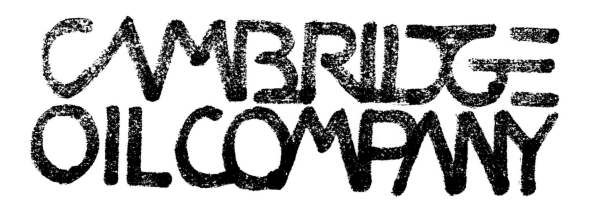

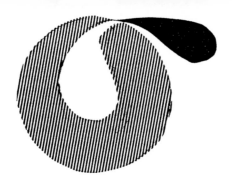

The second approach was more visual, using oil drops to symbolize the oil industry. We also tried the idea of repeating one shape to suggest continuity and flow, which also indicated the fact that the company is involved in various business concerns. We were thinking of applying the logo to gas stations, trucks, so the logo had to be visually strong and easy to remember. Our client liked both ideas but wanted a more corporate solution.

We combined the "C" and the shape of the drop in one image using two colors.

We tried another angle using the company initials to form a square, while retaining the idea of the drop by placing it inside the letter "O." Our client was not totally satisfied with the design, so we tried to modify it by using only two units, the "C" and "O." We were using two colors, one for the letters and one for the drop. We placed an outline around the design, instead of using colors, and our client was happy. We thought this would be the final logo. It was gold embossed on the company folder. But, we then realized that if we joined the two parts of the logo, it would make a more unified statement. Although the client liked the other version, he agreed to go with the new logo. This logo has been widely acclaimed, and has won awards.

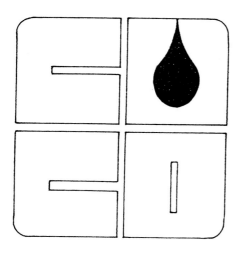
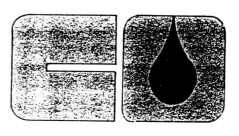

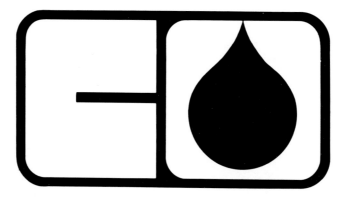

Designer: Itzhak Beery New York, New York
Client: Cambridge Oil Company

This logo is for Mike Quon Design Office, Inc., the first of the Quon brothers logos, designed 13 years ago. It still remains one of my favorite designs because it is very recognizable and tells the story. The design criteria was to communicate, in a design fashion, his profession (design and illustration). And, it has stood the test of time.

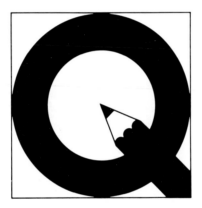

Designer: Mike Quon, New York, New York
Client: Mike Quon

The assignments to do logos for two brothers—one a dentist, the other a pharmacist—gave me a great opportunity to design an overall family look with a certain sense of humor.

I was given complete freedom, and since the brothers were going to use them mainly in a personal capacity, I didn't have to worry about advertising considerations. I just tried to pick out the most obvious images in their respective fields, and tried to make a "Q" out of them. Curiously enough, the ideas "cooked" in my head for quite a long time before I put anything on paper.

The assignment was to create a logo that gave desired information about Dr. Jeff Quon. The pharmacist's practice was to be symbolized with the letter "Q"—like the other two brothers. The project was approached with a certain sense of humor. After trying to turn the mortar and pestle into a "Q" shape, we decided it was too hard to read as a top view.

Approach with pill investigated like a clock, i.e., "it's time to take a pill".

In Greek mythology, a snake symbolizes life giving powers. The use of the snake in medicine is too evil looking.

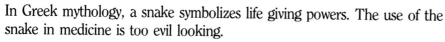

Mortar and pestle — this side view never worked.

Fun approaches, two faces; just kidding.

Pill and bottle.

240

Pill forms.

Tablet and pill forming "Q." "Q" with pill as the tail was finally decided upon.

Designer: Mike Quon, New York, New York
Client: Dr. Jeff Quon, Pharmacist

This assignment was for a logo for Dr. Timothy Quon, D.D.S.

The logo solution was chosen after deciding that the tooth was the most universal image for a dentist. Wanting to create a "Q" we had only to work out the tail for the letter. The graphic toothbrush seemed to solve the problem the best and create a positive feeling for a dentist. (I found that most people hate dentists. They give pain.)

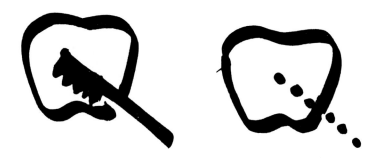

A toothbrush and tooth and the tooth theme, with red dots leading to a cavity.

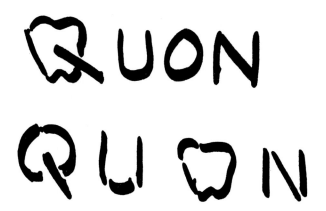

Interjecting tooth as letterform in the name.

Diagram, moving arrow approach.

Mirror in open mouth with teeth.

Arrows to form tail of "Q."

This idea carried over from Jeff Quon.

Supposed to be teeth and toothbrush.

Toothpaste and toothbrush — a less corporate, more design approach was tried.

These approaches are rather self-explanatory and, with the exception of the final design, left unexplored.

The final solution is a tooth and toothbrush not obviously a "Q" until paired with the other Quon brothers logos.

Designer: Mike Quon, New York, New York
Client: Dr. Timothy Quon, D.D.S.

This project involved developing a name recognition and service.

Rough concept of insulation

Adding tree to develop name recognition

Symbol and type sketch

Symbol and type alternate

Designer: LeeAnn Brook, Nevada City, California
Client: Timberline Insulation Company

This project was to create a logo for a private nutrition counseling practice that would depict the sciences as well as nutrition.

Getting initial concept on paper: apple in a medicine bottle and trial type design

Furthering graphic concept: apple in chemistry flask

Type arrangement   Further type arrangement   Final rough design

Designer: LeeAnn Brook, Nevada City, California
Client: The Berkeley Nutrition Group

The most difficult logo to design is one's own letterhead. The reason for this is the difficulty one has in being objective about oneself. However, after many indecisions, I arrived at a design that utilized my initials.

I thought that by using my initials, the logo would be more personalized.

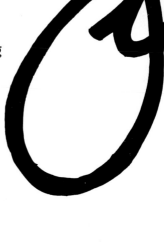

In my first attempt, I combined my initials with some lines which formed an enclosed box. After long thought, this seemed too confining; so I allowed the letters to be more flowing like one's own signature.

At this point I knew I had a good basic design from which to work. Using the logo in figure two as my nucleus, I expanded the letterhead to incorporate a piece of art identifiable with the commercial art field. After combining the repro pen with the typography, I was elated to find that they would work.

The last step was to refine the rough shown in figure three to the final logo shown in figure four.

Designer: Joseph D. Waller, Somerdale, New Jersey
Client: Joseph D. Waller

247

We were commissioned by our client, Consolidated Medical Equipment, Inc., a medical device manufacturer, to create a corporate mark. We were advised that they were known as "Conmed," but would still like to have their "official" name work well with the final mark.

We began working drawings, using the two words "conmed."

After more investigation into the product line, we found that the electrodes, their leading product, was designed with "a one-piece constructed center post of silver/silver chloride," as opposed to their competitors, who use two-piece construction, ie.: "children's pajama type snaps."

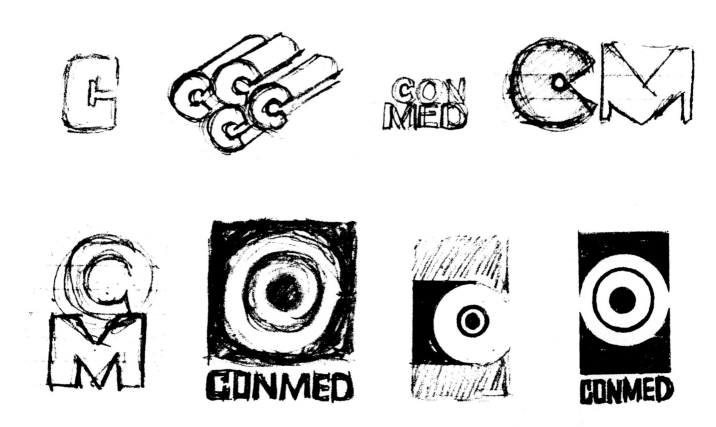

This center post is the connecting device to a cable, which enables a physician to get an accurate "reading" of a patient's EKG. So, we began sketches based on the top view on an electrode and center post.

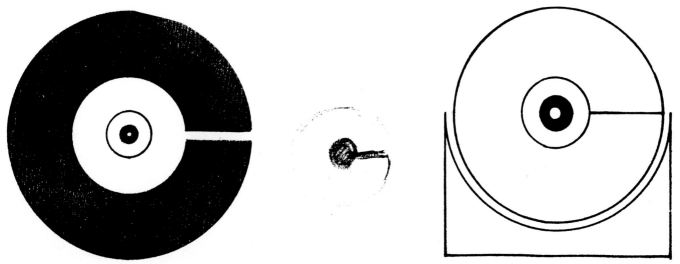

We stylized the top view of the electrode, and combined it with "conmed." Through research we found added symbolism—a triangle for delta means warning or be alert. This is exactly what electrodes should do; alert or warn the doctor of any problems in the patient.

The final version is used throughout all our communications packaging, advertising etc. Note: we used PMS 313 blue because of its "hospital" like color for our corporate color.

Designer: Don Romanelli, Clinton, New York
Client: Consolidated Medical Equipment, Inc.

Frank Omann, owner of Omann and Company Hair Designs, required a
new logo to coincide with a change in location and name.

Omann&COMPANY
H A I R   D E S I G N S

As his budget was very limited, we decided to start with a logotype development instead of a logo.

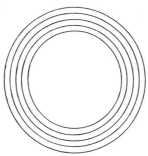

No preliminary sketches were presented to the client — only the final solution, with which we were all very pleased.

Omann & Company
hair designs

Full Service Salon for Men & Women

206 Pioneer Building
Telephone: 222.0061

Once this was agreed upon as a viable solution, the "curl" concept was introduced as a natural progression of thought and, consequently, the final
version of the logo.

Designer: The Design Company, Saint Paul, Minnesota
Client: Omann and Company Hair Designs

Silver & Harting and Company, Real Estate Developers, Philadelphia, PA, commissioned Noble Design Associates to design their new logo and graphic identity.

In reviewing the original design, it was very "horsey" and overpowering. We found there was lack of expression and sensitivity.

In talking with the clients and discussing their vision, it became clear that they wanted a quiet corporate design with a creative electric flair expressing their personality. Out of this meeting came the lightning bolt idea.

It was then developed and refined. This design was closer but still wasn't it.

SILVER⚡HARTING

Then there was the idea of using the negative space of the ampersand as the lightening bolt. A change from cap block lettering to a light serif upper and lower face created the welcoming feeling. The rest fell into place.

This final design gives a Japanese flavor and expresses integrity, balance and simplicity, which well represents Silver & Harting and Company.

Designer: Linda Noble, Philadelphia, Pennsylvania
Client: Silver & Harting and Company

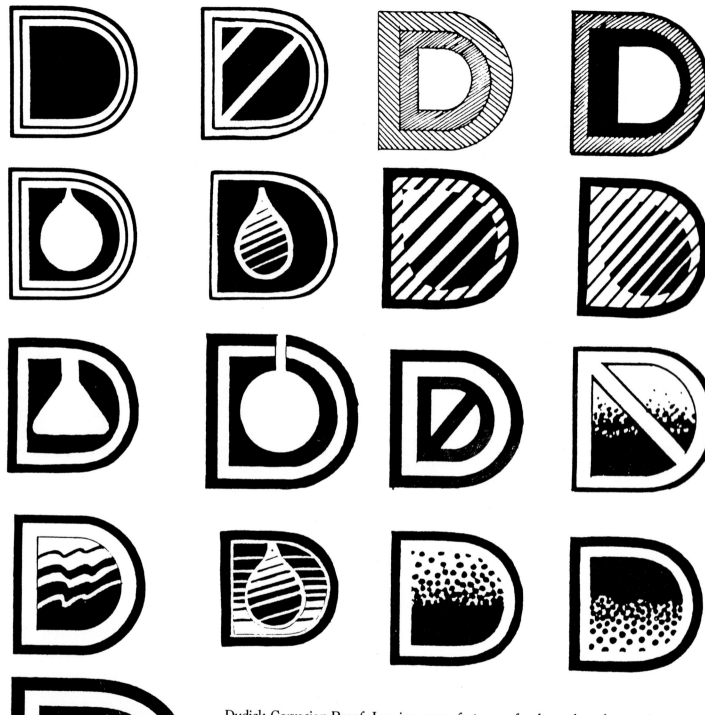

Dudick Corrosion-Proof, Inc. is a manufacturer of polymer-based corrosion proofing materials.

The original effort was an attempt to create an abstract symbol by combining the letterform "D" with the idea of corrosion containment.

The outer band defines the shape of the "D" while representing a protective coating that will contain the corrosion.

ORIGINAL LOGO

The client, however, wanted to retain some connection with the original Logotype. Some attempts were made to keep the imagery of corrosion part of the identifier, but it became evident that the best solution was a simple modification of the original mark. The refinements greatly improved the identifier's readability and reproduction quality, while fulfilling our original objective to show the confinement of corrosion by use of a protective coating.

Fortunately, the corrosive pattern used in the first solution was later adapted for use as a pattern element in Dudick's product catalog.

Designer: Walter M. Herip Design Assoc., Hudson, Ohio
Client: Dudick Corrosion-Proof, Inc.

The Cross Dental Care name and logo is a product of almost three years of careful deliberation and study on the part of the client to determine the exact nature of the image it required for marketing this dental service.

Progressive Dental Health Care

DENTAL CARECENTERS

A very corporate-IBM look was what the client insisted upon since the marketing was going to be directed towards working professionals with a "higher discretionary income."

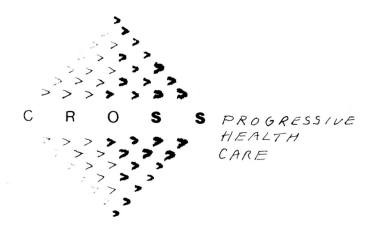

A great deal of effort was put into developing the name "Cross" so a logotype rather than a logo was requested. Nothing "cute" or remotely suggestive of teeth was to be presented. There were three phases of development. The first was to establish a visual direction.

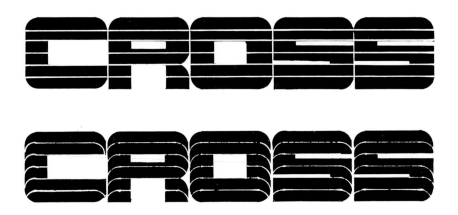

The above images were preferred designs, although simplification was needed in all cases.

In the second presentation there developed a definite look that the client liked — development of a distinctive typeface and treatment of the letterforms.

From this point the typeface was proportioned and refined, and a final layout/treatment was developed with which both the client and the designers were very pleased.

In the stationery format, the ruled lines are gold foil stamped.

Designer: The Design Company, Saint Paul, Minnesota
Client: Cross Dental Care Systems

This is a diversified company dealing in oil investments and large commercial real estate holdings.

TEXAS INFINITY CORPORATION

TEXAS INFINITY CORPORATION

TEXAS INFINITY
CORP.

TEXAS INFINITY CORP.

Designer: Nash Hernandez, Dallas, Texas
Client: Texas Infinity Corporation

The Jewish Board of Family and Children Services is a social organization operating for over 60 years. It has a long tradition of helping people with health, family, and mental problems. They commissioned us to update their logo and corporate identity because they wanted to appeal to young people of today. The object was to show an old reliable program with a contemporary face. In our initial designs we used simple images of children, family, and a family tree, to suggest long life and security.

Images of grouped people or children in a circle to indicate continuity, mutual help and understanding.

Our client liked the image of a group of three; a family.

To the three circles representing the heads, we added two pairs of enveloping arms, but the image appeared bottom-heavy and complicated.
We removed one pair of arms to simplify the image and designed the arms so that the reversed image would show the lower half of the Star-of-David, the Jewish symbol.

Thus, the motifs of family, care and Judaism are all represented, while the image is simple and modern.

We chose a classic typeface, Weiss, to balance the modern design and to show that the program was a combination of old and contemporary. The Weiss typeface fit our client's image perfectly and was subsequently used by us for all their publications.

Designer: Itzhak Berry, New York, New York
Client: Jewish Board of Family and Children Services

The assignment for the Summit Hotel was to create a logotype.

I approached this by depicting the upward sweep this name implies, at the same time trying to maintain a sophisticated look.

Designer: Nash Hernandez, Dallas, Texas
Client: The Summit Hotel

This assignment was for a logo development for Steve Lim Productions.

The client is involved in TV/Film production. Later on in the project, the client explained that he was also getting involved in the artwork side of filmmaking—storyboarding and cartooning. So we now were able to combine a film and art theme.

We started with names, letterforms and graphics. We approached it in a wide variety of design formats — taking advantage of the film idea. When the artwork theme became a design consideration, the logo, combining film and art, began to naturally evolve into the letter "L" for Lim. The client and designer then abandoned other solutions in favor of the final candidate.

This approach rather obvious. Use of film sprockets on bottoms of letters. Letterforms are too massive.

Another approach: a little corny. I like the motion generally.

This approach using the two names and has an interesting positive/negative effect.

Freehanded look. First letter with film sprocket holes was also considered.

The Chinese chop signature look related to company's heritage.

This approach with block designed lettering also related to oriental look.

This approach again reminded us of other existing companies.

We wanted a feeling of a stable, modern company. This began to look like we'd seen it before.

Too fashion oriented.

This one had good possibilities—liked the idea.

Supposed to be an "L". The first hint of a possible finished version.

Not right balance — just didn't feel right.

After the decision to incorporate the artwork aspect of company the idea started working itself out: combination of film and art. Film/art along with letterform for Lim.

Not pencil-like enough.

Too heavy. We liked square sprocket holes better.

The final logo gave the stable look we wanted, and outside gave information about what the company was involved with.

Steve Lim Productions
842 North Stanley Avenue
Los Angeles, California 90046
Phone (213) 655-1777

Steve Lim

Designer: Mike Quon, New York, New York
Client: Steve Lim Productions

This project was to develop a contemporary logo for a retail clothing store featuring jeans that could portray an image as well as name recognition.

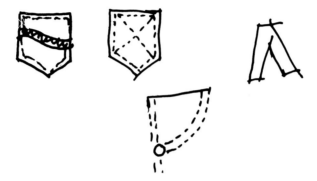

Getting possibilities/concepts on paper

Lettering development

Combining concept and lettering

Designer: LeeAnn Brook, Nevada City, California
Client: The Jeans Store

The Well Being, sponsored by Scripps Memorial Hospitals, is a health education center dedicated to promoting wellness. What could be a stronger image of wellness than an apple?

Various possibilities were pursued . . . whole apples with shiny spots, solid apples, linear apples, half-eaten apples with teeth marks . . . until a strong, simple shape of an apple was agreed upon, and a colorful symbol was developed as an identifying image for the The Well Being. The colors used are red for the apple, brown for the stem and green for the leaf.

The symbol has become a vital part of various marketing and promotional materials, as well as the signing.

Souvenir was chosen for the logotype due to its "organic" feeling. It relates much better to the apple than other typefaces that were under consideration.

WELL🍎BEING

Ugh! But had to try it.

WELL🍎BEING

Outline on apple helping. I don't know, I like it without it better. Too heavy here.

WELL🍎BEING

Tried Souvenir — much more organic than Helvetica below, relates better to form of apple.

Letterspacing much better — airy spacing feels a lot healthier! Letters can breathe, have a real sense of well-being.

WELL🍎BEING

Letterspacing too tight

WELL🍎BEING

Helvetica — too rigid, lifeless, boring, in contrast to "well-being — the state of being happy, healthy, or prosperous."

Well-being is a hyphenated word—therefore, the apple is between the two words.

Color helps, if possible; doesn't seem so heavy, feels happier in color; therefore, has a (once again) stronger sense of well-being.

I forgot to add leaf should flow upward (like a smile!) What a sense of well-being this leaf portrays.

The Well Being

The Well Being

We feel it is a positive symbol and fits in nicely in the environment of the shopping mall where The Well Being is located. It is the first center of its kind to be established by a hospital in a community shopping mall at the request of local citizenry.

Designer: HumanGraphic, San Diego, California
Client: The Well Being

Taracorp is an Atlanta-based refiner and processor. They requested a styliz-ed "T."

I started with a heavy bar treatment similar to the lead pigs and ingots Taracorp produces.

It seemed a bit heavy so I moved to a lower case version.

This needed some balance, so I mirrored the image. Now it was difficult to read as a "T."

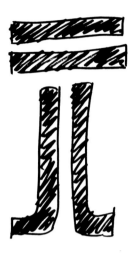

Merging upper and lower case produced this image. Solid, but too static.

Italicizing helped but top bars read too much like an "equals" sign.

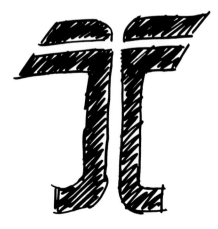

Close to the solution. Balanced, yet active from the bevel cut — but too heavy to integrate with type.

Outlining was the solution. The symbol is still bold, it integrates with type, and the open area inside the logo allows for second color application.

The alphabet followed naturally. Squarish in formation, as if machine-formed, the characters incorporated the bevel of the "T" logo. This alphabet is used throughout the corporate identity in division and product names. There are outline and italic versions in the alphabet for applications that require special emphasis.

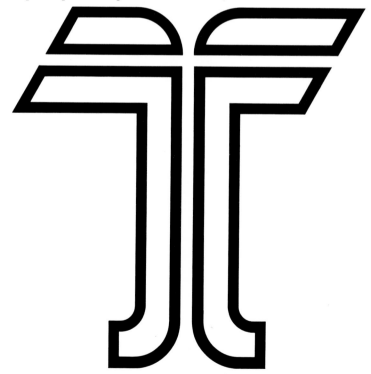

Designer: Brian Wood, Lithonia, Georgia
Client: Taracorp Industries .

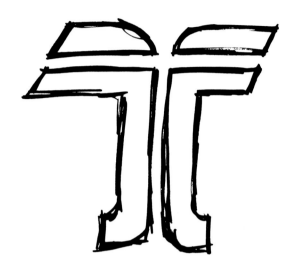

Final "T"

Incorporated with type treatment

Taracorp
Taramet
McCook
Park
Hoyt

Radiator solder promotion graphic

Product and manufacturing plants

Flexshield

Product names in typeface.

This project was to create a logo for a historic hotel that would have both a classic and contemporary look.

Initial lettering idea

Further lettering development

Sketch of the hotel's cupola for possible use in the logo

Incorporating the lettering and sketch of the copula

Possible alterations on final design

Designer: LeeAnn Brook, Nevada City, California
Client: The National Hotel

Alexander, Jr., Theodore C., 6283 N. Cicero Ave., Chicago, IL 60646

Ambrosino, Tom, Box 393, Neversink, NY 12765

Babcock & Schmid Associates, Inc., 3689 Ira Rd., Bath, OH 44210

Berry Associates Inc., Advertising Design, 101 Fifth Ave., New York, NY 10013

Brook, Leeann, Leeann Brook Design, The Ghidotti Building, 417 Broad St., Suite C, Nevada City, CA 95959

Bullock, David and Nora, graphic design/illustration, 617 Luella Drive, Kutztown, PA 19530

Carlin, Adrienne Y., AYC Graphics, 145 East 32nd St., New York, NY 10016

Carter Corporate Communications, Inc., David E., 1505 Carter Ave., Ashland, KY 41101

Connelly, Don, 108 N. Avondale Rd., P.O. Box 536, Avondale Estates, GA 30002

Daugherty, Patrick, Kneapler/ Daugherty, Package/Graphic/Corporate Design, 215 East Twenty-Ninth St., Suite 64, New York, NY 10016

Davis, Gene, Gene Davis & Associates Inc., 160 Roy St., Seattle, WA 98109

Follis and Associates, John, 2124 W. Venice Blvd., Los Angeles, CA 90006

Gayton, Silvio, Garber & Goodman Advertising Services Inc., 3550 Biscayne Blvd., Miami, FL 33137

Giordano Design, Ciro, 343 Salem St., Wakefield, MA 01880

Hartung & Associates, LTD., Graphic Design, 12919 Alcosta Blvd., Suite 4, San Ramon, CA 94583

Herip Design Assoc., Walter M., Turner's Mill, 36 East Streetsboro, Hudson, OH 44236

Hernandez, Nash, Nash Hernandez Graphic Design, Inc., 1140 Empire Central Dr., Suite 200, Dallas, TX 75247

Kaufman, Patricia Hayes, The Design Co., 265 Fort Rd., St. Paul, MN 55102-2438

Kneapler, John, Kneapler/Daugherty, Package/Graphic/Corporate Design, 215 East Twenty-Ninth St., Suite 64, New York, NY 10016

Leidel, Mike, John H. Harland Co., P.O. Box 105250 Atlanta, GA 30348

McKinney, Debbie, John H. Harland Co., P.O. Box 105250, Atlanta, GA 30348

Miller, Allan, 614 Fifth Ave., Suite C, San Diego, CA 92101

Noble, Linda, Noble Design Associates, 155 Arch St., Philadelphia, PA 19106

Pattinian, Merri Mechanick, Pattinian Design Studio, 7894 Dagget St., Suite 104, San Diego, CA 92111-2386

Porter Advertising, Tissa, P.O. Box 3931, Bryan, TX 77805

Quon, Mike, 53 Spring St., New York, NY 10012

Reynolds, Thomas H., T.H. Reynolds Advertising, 201 E. Fireweed Lane, Anchorage, AK 99503

Romanelli, Donald F., Advertising/Design, 2 College St., Clinton, NY 13323

Rosentswieg, Gerry, The Graphic Studio, 1509 North Cresent Heights Blvd., Los Angeles, CA 90046

Sonderman, Joe, Design/Joe Sonderman, Inc., 1209 Kenilworth Ave., Charlotte, NC 28204

Taylor, Pat, 3540 S St. N.W., Washington, D.C. 20007

Tscherny, Inc., George, 238 East 72 St., New York, NY 10021

Wagstaff, Jane Burton, Marketing by Design Inc., 716 Alhambra Blvd., Sacramento, CA 95816

Waller, Joseph D., 39 South Browning Road, Somerdale, NJ 08083

Weller, Don, The Weller Institute, 2427 Park Oak Drive, Los Angeles, CA 90068

Woo, Calvin, HumanGraphic, 3329 First Ave., San Diego, CA 92103

Wood, Brian, 1918 Panola Rd., Lithonia, GA 30058

Yoshikawa, Joy, The Design Co., 265 Fort Rd., Saint Paul, MN 55102-2438